'Goldrood'

The History of a Quaker Family

by

Joan Jackman

Edited by
David J. Miller

Published by

Abernant Publishing
Alltmawr Fach
Builth Wells
Powys LD2 3LJ

Printed and bound
in the United Kingdom by

Think Ink Fine Art Printers
11-13 Philip Road
Ipswich
Suffolk IP2 8BH

Copyright © 2012 Joan Jackman
ISBN: 978-1-909196-05-6
First published 2013

Preface – My Quaker Ancestry

For a number of years I have intended to produce this book, a history of a Quaker family. My other interests have taken over, Teaching, Gymnastics, the local Community and the Parish Council, but at 86 I must get down to it!

The history of my family can be traced back to William Alexander in 1591, James Corder 1640 and Francis Marriage 1656.

The family has always kept many records of their beliefs, their family trees, marriage certificates, business interests and most interesting of all – the paintings and drawings of Mary Ann Alexander, my great grandmother, which are reproduced within this book.

As the eldest grandchild living in this country, I wrote to every cousin suggesting that the most sensible solution would be to leave these records and illustrations, (rather than divide them up), to the Society of Friends, where they would be valued, looked after and friends and relations could access these in London.

When this story is completed this is how, with all the documentary detail, it will be housed - I hope you will enjoy reading it.

I must give many credits. Without the help of friends and colleagues this book would never have been completed.

John Grace - who has done a tremendous amount of family research.

Glenn Horridge - who has made my publishing arrangements.

Verity Trevor-Morgan - who has helped throughout with the intricacies of typing, recording, photography etc.

Sally Bayley - who checked and proofread for me.

Gill Ensoll - who typed many sections and deciphered my handwriting.

John Bamant - who offered historical advice.

'Timeless Images' - photographers of Bridgwater.

To the countless people who were interested enough to keep articles regarding 'Banking', 'Milling', 'Drapery' in Ipswich and for much help from the County Records Office.

V. Joan Jackman

Contents

QUAKER HISTORY 7

THE ALEXANDER FAMILY 10

THE CORDER FAMILY 15

THE MARRIAGE FAMILY 19

THE HOUSE OF GOLDROOD 24

THE DIARY AND TRAVELS OF MARY ANNE - 1849 42

TEN DAYS IN THE ISLE OF WIGHT 55

NOW FOR OUR LONG TALKED OF HOLIDAY IN SOUTH SHIELDS..61

MARIANNE CORDER - A FEW MEMORIES OF A LONG LIFE 68

THE STORIES OF HERBERT AND BERNARD MARRIAGE 92

PERSIS IN AMERICA AND NURSING IN FRANCE 102

GERARD AND ARTHUR MARRIAGE 107

Quaker History

George Fox, founder of the Quaker movement was born in Fenny Drayton, Leicester in 1624. He lived through a Civil War and was imprisoned by King and Parliament.

Many religious groups had arisen in England, Baptists, Anabaptists, Ranters, Levelers, Seekers, these all being small independent groups of thinkers who saw disunity in the Church, with worldly clergy more influenced by worldly ambition than religion.

George Fox moved around the country, meeting and uniting groups and clergymen. He set out to preach 'a message of spiritual honesty' and to speak out against the religious turmoil which existed in this country. Many people were ready and eager to listen to him and to spread his teachings. Thus many groups were set up all over the country, but their early preachings against "the vain customs of the world" did not meet with the approval of the established Church.

In his 'Journals or Historical Account of the Life Travels, Sufferings, Christian Experiences and Labour of Love in the Work of the Ministry' George Fox describes his travels all over Great Britain from Scotland, to Lands End, to Ireland and in Wales.

Many laws were made against Catholics and these often applied equally well to Quakers, but some were specific. In 1661 an 'Act for Preventing Mischiefs and Dangers that may arise by certain Persons called Quakers and others refusing to take Lawful Oaths' was passed. It was unlawful for more than five persons to gather together under Pretence of Worship. Many of the groups George Fox met on his travels were therefore in danger of persecution, many meetings were broken up and his followers imprisoned.

Quaker beliefs were strong and immovable and these put them in direct conflict with the Church and the Laws of the land. They refused to pay tithes or rates to the Church of England, would not make use of any Minister for wedding or burial, refused to fight, believed all men rich or poor to be equal and in this belief refused to doff their hats to anyone, whatever their station.

In most cases breaking the law was punished by fines but these were increased for persistent offenders. If fines were not paid, household goods or animals were forfeited and many Quakers were imprisoned for their beliefs. Over 4000 Quakers were imprisoned and some died as a result of their treatment.

In 1672 under Charles II, there was some relaxation of the laws and four hundred and ninety prisoners were released and pardoned and for a time the Penal laws were suspended but they were later reinforced.

When James II came to the throne in 1685, sufferings were lessened by a `Declaration for Liberty of Conscience`, Quakers preached against unnecessary celebration with meat, drink and ostentatious clothing. They dealt with those who did not attend meetings regularly and advised on the upbringing of children, saying parents should set an example to their children, and use plain language at all times. They should care for the poor and for those in their employ, and those employed as servants or governesses should also be Quakers, to be a good example for the children.

Quakers preached honesty, payment of debts, encouraged Friends' children to work for businesses run by other Friends. They encouraged charitable work. They spoke against frequenting ale houses and visiting fairs, games and side shows which encouraged noise and laughter and drunken behaviour.

The Quaker meetings had neither ministers nor religious rituals, they had no prepared sermons but any member of the congregation might be moved by the Spirit to speak. They addressed each other as `thee` or `thou` and refused to take any oath other than saying `yea` or `nay`. Because they were so savagely treated in this country many left for America, where William Penn founded the State of Pennsylvania in 1682.

Friends adopted a policy of non-violence, refusing to take part in war. In the First World War and the Second World War, they were recognised as Conscientious Objectors and were directed by the courts to work of peaceful national importance, such as in the mines or industry. Many however took part in non-violent sections of the war, driving ambulances or becoming stretcher bearers, nurses or hospital orderlies. Quaker relief services have been present in most disasters, organising relief, aiding refugees, administering supplies. They took a leading part in the abolition of slavery, prison reform (Elizabeth Fry) and better education. They founded the Quaker schools which were very early among the first co-educational boarding schools and were well known for their good treatment in their workplaces such as Cadbury's, Fry's, Clarks, Banking and Biscuit Factories.

This letter was written in 1840 to illustrate the language by which Quakers wrote to each other:

'Thank you for the very kind and agreeable invitation to pass a few days at your home when we come to London to attend the yearly meeting which we quite hope to do. I think thou said'st either before or after the meeting.

I should be pleased to have a letter from thee as we shall hope to meet again before long. Give my love to Isabella and accept it thyself, my Dear Mary from thy sincere friend.'

Ellen M Alexander

The Alexander Family

At first, the Alexander family had been Church of England and when they moved from Hampshire, their son was Rev John, a C of E Vicar. The first of the family to become a Quaker was William Alexander who lived in Needham in 1681. He was sent to the County gaol for preaching Quaker beliefs, was fined £5.00 and sent back to gaol for refusing to pay.

From then on the family became a staunch and well respected Quaker family.

Alexander Family Tree (direct descendants)

Thomas Alexander   married   > Elizabeth Habershon

Rev John   > Elizabeth Tyler

William 16.. - 1706   > Grace Farthing
The first to become a Quaker

Samuel 16.. - 1732   > Martha Dikes

Samuel 1716 - bachelor
Founder of Needham Market Bank 1774

Dykes 1724 - 1786   > Martha Biddle 1726 - 1775
Nephew, who carried on the Bank

Samuel 1749 - 1824   > Elizabeth Gurney 1747 - 1786
Nephew

Samuel 1773 - 1838   > Rebecca Biddle 17..- 1849

Samuel and Rebecca had twelve children, eleven of whom lived. Mary Ann Alexander (the Diarist) was the ninth of these children who, in 1850 married Henry Shewell Corder. They had two children, Henry (1855 - 1944) and Marianne (1857 - 1947). Mary Ann died in 1913 aged 98 years.

East Anglian Bank History

The Alexanders were mainly ship owners, engaged in the iron and corn trades and had a Corn business in Woodbridge, but branched successfully into the Banking business where they were much respected.

The grandson of William, Samuel born 1716 having worked in the Ipswich Bank, founded Needham Market Bank in 1774. He was a bachelor and his banking business was carried on by his two nephews, Samuel 1749 - 1824 and Dykes 1724 - 1824.

Banking continued to be the Alexander family business passing to other members of the family. Dykes' son Samuel Alexander 1773 - 1838, was educated at a classical school in Reading and spent the rest of his life in Ipswich, entering his father's bank at the age of 15. He became a partner in the bank but resigned on health grounds aged 40 and then devoted the rest of his life and monies with the Society of Friends and assisting in founding many benevolent societies – the Anti-Slavery, Bible and Peace Society and various educational movements. He was passionately involved in the Temperance Movement and built, at his own expense, The Temperance Hall in High Street, Ipswich.

Samuel lived in a house where the London and Norwich roads divide and now is the eastern end of Clarkson Street. New streets in Ipswich in 1865 were named in honour of anti-slavery campaigners, Wilberforce, Clarkson and Benezet. Benezet was an American Quaker who spent much money in the cause of American Negro freedom. He also wrote many treatise on the subject.

A list of Suffolk subscribers for the Temperance tracts is shown in the Suffolk Museum as well as an account of their work in South Africa. Richard Dykes Alexander writing to a Roman Catholic priest in Northern Ireland, Theobald Matthew, with an account of progress in Ireland "Drunkenness will never again with Divine Assistance become the National Sin of Ireland".

In 1848, there is an account of the first Temperance Society in Russia. "Unhappily this has been discouraged by the Government and we hear the little society has been crushed in its infancy. We may hope for better days." Sara Biller.

In 1831 Ann Alexander has a letter from her brother-in-law in London, Dr John Sims, on his work with the spread and medical treatment of Cholera, which was spreading throughout the country and was very bad in some country areas where little medical care was available. In 1838 Dr

Sims and his wife both died and his two orphaned children were brought up by Richard Dykes and wife Ann Alexander of Ipswich.

William, who they brought up, was apprenticed to a milling firm in Chelmsford and in 1845 was appointed to a Quaker firm as a cashier, Ransomes and May. This later became Ransomes and Sims, makers of agricultural machinery. A partner in the firm, John Head, whilst travelling in Russia, wrote to his partner justifying carrying firearms contrary to Quaker principles.

"With respect to the pistol I have not brought it with me as I shall have no occasion to leave Odessa, but altho' I am a member of the Society of Friends and I believe many of their doctrines are right ones, NOTHING would induce me to travel to the interior of Russia, night or day, without firearms. It is not often you require to use them, but at the very sight of a revolver, or the knowledge that you have one in your possession, will deter most of the natives from making an attack on you ------ I have never used the pistol but once and that was one night when some men attacked us who wanted to steal our luggage from behind the carriage. Directly they saw we were armed and heard a ball whizzing over their heads, they bolted as fast as their legs would carry them. Believe me ---- our business abroad calls me to do many things which are not in direct accordance with our doctrines as members of the Society of Friends."

This was a time of great progress in agriculture and the firm of Ransome and Sims, based in Chelmsford, travelled to Poland and Hungary, Russia and Austria.

In 1808 Dykes Alexander bought an isolated country cottage built by a Mr Head in 1799, on land known as 'Golden Rood' or 'Goldrood' and in 1809 this was bought by Samuel Alexander who built his country mansion on this land, with covenants prohibiting the erection of obstructions to the River Orwell view. He and his wife Rebecca Biddle, moved in, in 1811, and brought up their twelve children there. He died in 1838 and Rebecca in 1849, when the family were still living at Goldrood. One of the sad pictures of Mary Ann's book is of 'moving day' when they packed up and left the house. (Mary Ann, the diarist and painter in this book, was my great grandmother.)

An interesting story is told of the Ipswich bank in 1822. Bank notes were being carried by mail coach from London to Ipswich by a member of the firm. He placed a parcel in a locker under his seat and pocketed the key. He left the coach at Colchester for a short time, but when he returned his three travelling companions had disappeared and when he reached

Ipswich found his bank notes had also vanished. Ipswich Bank then offered the following reward of £1000 which was later raised to £5000.

£1000 Reward, Alexander & Co

Stolen from the Ipswich Mail on its way from London to Ipswich on the night of Sept. 11th 1822. Stolen £31,199 in notes.

Ipswich Bank have therefore issued the following notes. £5.00 & £10.00

Manningtree Bank £1.00, £5.00, £10.00
Alexander & Co and Fry & Co
Hadleigh Bank £1.00, £5.00, £10.00

Whosoever gives information leading to the apprehension of the stolen property shall receive the above reward

£5000 Reward, Alexander & Co

Not having obtained their parcel of notes taken from the mail on Sept 11th, Alexander & Co have circulated a new issue of notes.

Any notes printed in RED accept
Any notes printed in BLACK reject

Ipswich & Needham Banks
Woodbridge & Hadleigh Banks
Printed in BLACK accept

Whosoever gives information leading to the conviction of the thieves shall receive £5,000. But without the recovery of the property £2,000.

The greater part of the notes were afterwards recovered by negotiation with the thieves' solicitors.

The Alexanders continued their banking enterprises and other members of the family became partners. They continued as members of the Society of Friends and gave much time to the works of the town of Ipswich and neighbourhood. W H Alexander re-arranged the Town Library. He was a Town Councillor and Alderman of the Borough.

Frederick Alexander carried on the business near St Mary Key Church, known as Bank Street and lived at Woodbridge Bank. He was local Treasurer of the British and Foreign Bible Society.

Mr William S Gurney became a partner in the Ipswich Bank and under the partnerships of W Alexander, W S Gurney, R Kerrison and H Birkbech the banks amalgamated with Barclay and Company Ltd.

The Corder Family

The first recorded Corders are from the early 1600s with James Corder 1640 - 1710 and Elizabeth Firebrace 16.. - 1704. They were married in 1665 and lived in Pebmarsh, Essex. They were members of the Church of England and had seven children.

The youngest of these children was Michael 1680 - 1766 and he became the first Quaker in the family at the age of 21. He married twice, Elizabeth Plasted and in 1711 Elizabeth Woodwards 16.. - 1748.

Michael and Elizabeth Woodwards had one son Micah, married to Mary Foster and their son married Ruth Marriage from another Quaker family.

Corder Family Tree

James Corder		> Elizabeth Firebrace
Michael 1680 - 1766 (First of the Corder family to become a Quaker)		> Elizabeth Woodwards
Micah 1712 - 1782		> Mary Foster 17.. - 1760
John 1758 - 1829		> Ruth Marriage 1760 - 1815
Thomas 1780 - 1833		> Mary Shewell
Henry Shewell Corder 1814 - 1912	1st marriage	> Rachel Spence (died)
	2nd marriage	> Mary Ann Alexander (Painter and Diarist) 1815 - 1913

They had two children: Henry 1855 - 1944 and Marianne 1857 - 1947

Henry Corder moved to Bridgwater and founded Corder's Seed Merchants on the Cornhill, Bridgwater.

Marianne Corder married Herbert Marriage, my grandfather, and they had twelve children.

Tavern Street Front of Frederic Corder & Son Ltd

The Corder family remained staunch members of the Society of Friends and were known in Ipswich not only as successful business men but also as public spirited men doing much voluntary service. They were mainly associated with the firm of `Shewell and Corder` later to become `Frederic Corder & Son Ltd`, a draper's shop in 18 Tavern St, Ipswich, which later expanded through to the Butter Market. The Tavern Street front of Messrs Corders' premises remained almost unaltered for over 100 years being replaced in 1926.

The firm was founded in about 1787 and celebrated its 150th anniversary on January 22nd 1937 when the East Anglian magazine wrote its story in `Story of East Anglian Businesses' tracing its history and that of its proprietors.

A number of the Corder family served as apprentices there, serving seven years unpaid and described by Henry Shewell Corder as having to work from 7am till 9 pm every day and sometimes till midnight with no half day off. He left and worked for a time in North Shields and then returned as a partner, until he left the shop due to ill health and went to farm with his brother at Fyfield Hall Farm.

He married his second wife, Mary Anne Alexander at Needham Market, Suffolk in 1850. Mary Ann was the artist and diarist much of whose work is shown in this book. They had two children Henry and Marianne Corder. Henry lived from 1855 - 1944 and Marianne 1857 – 1947.

Henry Shewell Corder & Mary Ann (Alexander) Corder on his 90th birthday

Henry the eldest, set up a business in Bridgwater, Somerset - a seed and corn merchant at the Cornhill and he and his wife Alice lived there and brought up two boys. Henry Corder was a committed Quaker who worshipped in the Meeting House in Friarn Street and frequently preached at the Sunday meetings. He was an avid collector of many interesting items – birds' eggs, shells, fossils, was very interested in astronomy and gave many lectures at local schools.

Parties at Uncle Harry's house were hard work. Whereas at other parties, pictures were up on the walls showing well known adverts - Ovaltine, Bovril etc which you had to identify, here 'The Cathedrals of England' were pinned up!

His younger sister Marianne married Herbert Marriage and they had twelve children. They lived in Essex but when Herbert died, Marianne moved to Burnham-on-Sea with the younger children, who went to Sidcot

- the Quaker School in Somerset. They called their new home in The Grove, Burnham - 'Goldrood' after their old house.

It is rather sad to realise that the whole family were never all together. Marianne was a cripple, born with a dislocated hip, (not operable in those days). Whilst Marianne was at home bringing up the family, Herbert travelled three times to Canada, setting up his sons in this rugged country, which offered great new experiences for those able to work and homestead in this exciting venture. They all made some visits home bringing their families.

Many of the family remained members of the Quaker faith, anti-war, yet serving as stretcher bearers in the First World War, nursing in France, working in hospitals. And in recent years were frequently found volunteering when emergencies occurred in many parts of the world.

The Marriage Family

The family are believed to have come as Huguenot refugees from Valenciennes in NE France and the earliest recorded name is Francis Marriage 16.. - 1706 and his wife Mary 16.. -1712.

Francis was a farmer living at Holts Farm near Stebbing, Essex. He was first known as a Friend having met and listened to George Fox. He was an outspoken follower and proceeded to travel around the countryside preaching Quakerism. For this he was twice imprisoned at Colchester Castle in 1659 and again later in 1660.

The Marriage Family direct descendents:-

Francis Marriage 16.. - 1701 > Mary 16.. - 1712

William 1668 - 1738 > Ruth Woodward 1690 - 1772

William 1725 - 1774 > Susannah Smith 1721 - 1777

John 1756 - 1816 > Mary Gopsill 17.. - 1807

John 1784 - 1849 > Rebecca Bootham 1788 - 1848

John 1810 - 1880 > Margaret Marriage 1809 - 1874

Herbert Marriage 1846 - 1904 > Marianne Corder 1857 - 1947

Twelve children:

Herbert, Bernard, Persis, Gerard, Arthur, Dorothy, Marjorie, Paul, Barbara, Irene, Monica and Anthony.

Dorothy Marriage married James Hughes Cornish and there were two children Joan and Audrey.

Joan Cornish married Richard Jackman

Audrey Cornish married Kenneth Broome

The family tree was first researched by Francis Corder Clayton and the 1857 tree updated to the `1921` tree. Paul Marriage of Newbury carried out further research to 1987 and found three other apparently unconnected Marriage families. In 1987 a Marriage Family Reunion was held at Broomfield Mill, Chelmsford, Essex when 203 Marriages and relatives were present.

The Hugenots were Protestants and during the 16th Century, Catholics and Protestants battled in religious turmoil. In August 1572, the Massacre of St Batholomew's Eve, 6000 men, women and children were murdered by Catholics.

This led to the exodus of French Protestants, many were welcomed to this country as they were skilled workmen and craftsmen. In particular they sought out areas where their skills were needed. One influential group settled in Appledore in North Devon. Here their skills were recognised in that wool producing area.

In general, members of the Marriage family were farmers and millers from around Chelmsford, Essex. William Marriage 1777 - 1824 was the first to become a miller. At one time the family and its descendants owned three windmills, six water mills and ten farms supplying wheat to the mills. The milling business was known as W & H Marriage & Sons Ltd.

The family business was that of milling and flour making. In England in the 1820s there were tens of thousands of windmills and water mills which made flour for the English population. The Marriages were staunch Quakers, religion was important in their business and their dealings with other members of the Community. They looked after their employees, both those who worked the farms and loved the countryside, the servants who ran the house and garden and those who helped with the upbringing of the children. We shall see later how towns and villages developed, often being built specifically for workers of one particular trade or industry, such as that of Clark's shoes or Cadbury's chocolate.

Early business history showed that the family business passed through a quarter of a century of misfortunes, bank failures, bad seasons and agrarian discontent. Reaping machines were practically unknown and corn was cut by scythes, hooks and sickles. Corn was thrashed by a flail. The first steam engine was made by J R and A Ransom's of Ipswich, in 1842, who were a well known Quaker family.

In 1815, the first Corn Laws were introduced to protect British land owners. During the Napoleonic Wars, no wheat came from abroad and prices were high but fell when foreign wheat entered the country. Agriculture employed 20% of the population at this time.

In 1845 a potato blight destroyed much of the Irish crop causing the Irish Potato Famine. In England, bread was the staple diet of the poor but in Ireland, it was potatoes. The repeal of the Corn Laws was too late to save the Irish and it was estimated that at least one million died and another million emigrated.

In 1846 the repeal of Corn Laws marked a change in the agricultural industry in Great Britain and imported wheat began to come into the country from Russia and the United States of America.

In Norfolk, a system of crop rotation was introduced which helped to lighten the heavy soil of counties such as Essex. The opening of the railways had a big input into the agricultural industry, The Stockton - Darlington railway was financed by Quaker money and opened in 1825. Stephenson's Rocket was built at this time.

Edward Marriage developed a method of dressing flour with a silkmesh, superseding the use of a bolt of horse hair and exhibited this method and other mill products at The Great Exhibition of London in 1851, held in Hyde Park, for which he received a Diploma.

Finance was now opening up and becoming more available to farmers. In East Anglia regular banks were opening up. In Ipswich in 1767 and in 1783 a note is signed by Samuel Alexander, Emerson Cornwall and John Spooner, this was the Alexander family, ship owners, also engaged in the iron and corn trades. Other Quaker families, also influential in the banking world, were the Gurneys.

Wilson Marriage worked in Ireland having served his apprenticeship with his father and then returned to Colchester, leaving his father to devote himself to public work and to work on the Colne Harbour Commission, opening up the waterways which were the most economical method of moving foreign wheat. In a short time a second steam engine was added and in service from 1842 - 1873.

Family property was now extending in Ipswich, a dwelling house was built, a grocer's opened, a warehouse, candle factory, stables, sheds and the Jerusalem Coffee House opened.

The family were Quakers from their earliest beginnings and an amusing story is told of Henry Marriage, who in the course of bargaining with a local butcher for some beasts, the butcher used a swear word. Henry stopped the negotiations at once and ordered him to go and wash his mouth out at the cattle trough, before he would continue the deal!

The family continued as corn merchants but further diversification continued. In 1856, they bought up 2000 tons of coal, which was unloaded by casual labour, each man carrying baskets at 6^d a ton – and a free beer! How did this square with the Quaker temperance?

A new stock taking book of 1856 showed the following recordings:-

'Stocks in Mills and Farms £20,738.95 pence.

1857 - Bad debts have been few. Trade favourable.

We lost a number of horses and cows this year.

Damage at Moulsham Mill. £130 to set it right.

Lost 6 pretty good horses this year.

Good trade in oil cake. Lost many bullocks with lung complaint.

Sold £800 worth of cabbages in London market in 8 month period.'

But from 1875 onwards, flour from the Continent and N America was finding favour with the baking industry. A little wholemeal was still produced for brown bread and great efforts were being made to grow better wheat in this country.

Coat of Arms of the Marriage Family

By the Second World War, W & H Marriage were still in business and were further extended in 1957, but whilst local trade supported the nation's health food shops, specialised supermarkets took over, requiring mass production and national distribution.

The last great flour salesman is recorded as 'Percy' who travelled to London with his Gladstone Bag and a 1/- shilling all-day tram ticket. Percy was also known locally as a keen hunting man who was usually 'in at the kill'. He was said to know every short cut and hedge gap in Essex. He was still hunting at 85, and though often asleep in the saddle at the end of the day, his old horse always brought him home safely!

Memories of the Marriage family are still alive in Essex. Many are Quakers, they support Friends' Schools, though Goldrood, whilst still existing as a building, is now greatly altered and enlarged is now a boarding Catholic School.

The House of Goldrood

This is the story of a house called Goldrood, near Ipswich, built in 1811 by Samuel Alexander, a local banker, and shown in a series of watercolours, which his daughter, Mary Ann, drew and painted between 1840 and 1850.

This was a Quaker household and many of the paintings illustrate the ethos of the Quakers, or 'Friends', as they preferred to be called.

Samuel was a member of the Alexander family and he and many other families, particularly the Gurneys, did much to develop trade and industry in the 18th century and in particular the East Anglian Banks.

The house is recorded in the town history of 1351 and 1522 and various spellings and derivations of the name exist, from Goldenrood to Goldroyd and Gold Rood. Rood as in Rood Screen means 'Cross of Christ', from the Old English 'Rod' - cross or gallows.

In 1808, the land originally came into the family as a country cottage called Goldrood. Samuel Alexander bought it and built a country mansion in which he brought up his large and growing family.

The late John Cornforth wrote an article describing the drawings and paintings made by Mary Ann Corder (née Alexander) and lent by John Grace and the Marriage family. These are central to this chapter on the house of Goldrood.

A second book telling of the travels of Mary Ann, her younger sister Rebecca and brother John, on a visit to Guernsey, is also treasured by the family. This account has been my inspiration for other chapters later in my book.

The paintings of Mary Ann are interesting because they illustrate the influence of the family upbringing. The furnishing and decorations are in direct contrast with the grandeur of the house.

John describes Mary Ann's drawings as showing 'an unselfconscious charm' and though she would have had drawing lessons they would have been with a tutor or governess and not an established artist as was brought in by the Gurney family. She had certainly been taught good English and spellings. Her handwriting is beautiful and almost faultless, still very clear today. The family have a 'sampler' with the numbers one to ten, stitched when Mary Ann was nine years old in 1824.

As was the custom with Quakers, no musical instrument is seen in the house and she was unlikely to have been taught any music. Within the house, few pictures are shown on the walls and in the bedroom, only very small mirrors are evidenced.

Mary Ann was one of twelve children born to Samuel and Rebecca (nee Biddle). They were Sophia, Elizabeth, Ellen, Rachel, Samuel, John, George, Frederick, **Mary Ann**, Rebecca, Charlotte and Gurney.

Rebecca seems to have been the closest to Mary Ann. She was two years younger and profoundly deaf but was included in many of the paintings and travels, the only other named sibling is John, who went with his sisters to Guernsey.

The house of Goldrood overlooked a view down to the River Orwell (a view now unfortunately blocked by a housing estate). Its main feature is of the six domed windows overlooking the garden and which gave light to the dining room and above it, the drawing room.

May Ann liked to feature family and friends, the servants, gardeners and workers on the estate. Very frequently she included herself in the sketch, often the family pet dogs and other animals, but mainly in her first book, she draws every room in the house, showing kitchens, pantries, store rooms and bedrooms. Also shown are 'the Hermitage' or summerhouse, where the children played and another called 'The Swiss Cottage' in a walled part of the garden, with an elaborate greenhouse.

The dining room is obviously an important room and is pictured twice, once looking out into the garden and across to the view of the distant River Orwell, and the other showing the fireplace with their mother, Rebecca (née Biddle), sitting by the fire. Mary Ann is seated with her back to the door, with two others at the table. Mary Ann is without a headdress and the two on the couch are in bright coloured dresses and no head covering. This shows a difference in attitude even within families, some were known as plain and others were more relaxed in their attire. Rebecca was certainly not. She was always sombrely dressed and her bedroom is very plain with white hangings, a small mirror and plain chair and table. Mary Ann obviously loved colour, she spent much of her time drawing and painting and writing verse, but must have helped Rebecca overcome her extreme disability and they were very close.

The furnishing in the dining room shows a tapestry screen, always called by the family 'The Adam & Eve Screen' but sold by my uncle Henry Corder in about 1930. There are some ornaments shown on the mantelpiece and two long bell ropes beside the fire are to summon the servants. A small child is shown at the edge of the table and it appears that this was a room where the family often sat to read or sew and draw.

An interesting room is called 'The Museum'! It was a breakfast room but appears to have also been used as a school room. There are gold drape curtains at the windows, a red striped tablecloth and many wall hangings of maps and some pictures. Two large covered objects, one at each end of the room, may have been globes for showing geographical world features. The Victorians were great collectors and the drawers and glass fronted cabinets may well have housed collections of shells, dried pressed flowers, fossils, small rocks, pebbles, moths or butterflies, collected by family members. They were unlikely to have valued unnecessarily or show pleasure in decorations and there is no sign of fine art, but they often had collected prints or portfolios rather than framed pictures.

Where most paintings of Victorian rooms concentrate on the furniture, Mary Ann shows in great detail the workings of the house and garden. The back kitchen shows the sink, pots and pans, a large sieve and an open fire, with heavy pots on it. Mr Lockwood, seen in other paintings in the garden, is shown bringing in vegetables to Miss Fisk who, with a mixing bowl, is getting the food prepared. The contraption above the grate is to ring the bell to each living room.

Mr Lockwood was certainly a busy man, not only did he bring in the garden produce but he helped with the haymaking - (still with his top hat on!) which Mary Ann enjoyed sketching.

Another maid, H Dawson is pictured in the pantry. She appears to be doing some washing with a large jug of water beside the sink. Sets of blue cups and saucers, various jugs, pitchers and decorative china can be seen, and many cupboards and drawers beneath the working top are fitted right around the pantry, to provide ample storage space for such a large family collection of utensils and crockery.

One of the last family gatherings is shown in the dining room. This room was on the ground floor with a domed roof, a fireplace and full, coloured curtains. Here the difference in dress appears quite clear. Gurney, the youngest boy of the family, is first on the left, then two young girls in red and green. Rebecca, nearest the fireplace, has on a plain dark coloured dress. In front of the fire are two young men, then John seated by Mary Ann, is the brother who went to Guernsey with Mary Ann and Rebecca. Mary Ann is brightly dressed, whilst one of the older sisters and brother, to the right of the picture, appear to be plain and darkly dressed.

Rather sad is the 'moving day' picture when the family moved to a smaller home. The horse-drawn cart is shown laden with mattresses, chairs and buckets. The family dog - not sure what is happening - will he be left behind?

Samuel Alexander died in 1838 and his widow Rebecca, carried on as a partner in the bank with John Biddle until 1845, when she made way for her two sons. Rebecca died in 1849 and the remaining members of the family moved out as shown in the 'moving day' picture in 1850. They had many happy years at Goldrood and Mary Ann wrote "Oh! May their memory linger yet, where these bright scenes are part of all the blessings, that they hold, be with us to the last."

Goldrood: The Alexander Home

Dining Room: Grandmother seated by the fire. The Adam & Eve fire screen clearly visible

The Dining Room: Bow-windows looking out to the River Orwell

Rebecca Alexander's Bedroom

Front Room & Bedroom

Breakfast Room & School Room, with globes and maps

33

The Museum with cabinets showing collections

34

Back Kitchen with Mr Lockwood & Miss Fisk

The Pantry showing Miss Dawson doing some washing

Four children playing in The Hermitage

Mary Ann & Rebecca watching Mr Newsom & the haymakers

Mr Newsom outside the Front Door

Last Family Gathering

Departure from Goldrood

The Diary and Travels of Mary Anne - 1849

In her second book of water colours, Mary Ann wrote of her holiday in Guernsey with brother John and sister Rebecca, where they visited friends and relations. She was married at the end of 1850, and in 1851 writes of a trip she and Henry made to the Isle of Wight. In August 1854, they took the 'Long talked-of holiday to the dark and dismal town of Shields', where they visited friends and relations.

Included also are paintings, undated, showing the many places she visited, Scarborough, Scotland and Derbyshire, but nothing is written of these journeys. They would mostly appear to be with Rebecca and must have entailed long train journeys.

Guernsey - or - 'I can't get out'

Mary Ann wrote a preface to her story of her visit to Guernsey, in which she describes the beauty of the Island, the hospitality they received and yet compares it to the feeling of a caged bird, lovely beaches, long walks yet always the feeling of being trapped and not able to get out!

Guernsey - 1849

Suddenly it came into the mind of my brother John to visit Guernsey and as readily my sister Rebecca and myself fell in with his proposition to accompany him, notwithstanding our dread of a night voyage and on the 7th of the 9th month 1849 we were on the Pier at Southampton, watching a lovely sunset, when the Despatch steamer came alongside and we were soon on board partaking of a comfortable tea, conversing with our new acquaintances and watching with mingled curiosity and amazement, the various passing events of our new location.

We might have gathered a few hints with regard to comfort, from the dress of our fellow passengers, who had perhaps more experience in sea travelling than ourselves. One dress in particular struck us as peculiarly adapted for a cool Autumn night, as a lady buttoned up a double breasted great coat and then added to the singularity of her appearance by the addition of one of those comfortable yet not less ugly, shades to the front of the bonnet.

Our opposite neighbour, an old lady who, laying aside bonnet and cap at the same instant, showed a round cropped head to the evident amusement of many of the sitters. I for one, little thought when I gave way to my first smile, how pleasant a companion I should soon find her on the deck of the steamer, conversing, with various subjects of interest, touching on ragged schools, briefly on politics, on education in general as well as the unfolding of mind from earliest infancy to the truths contained in the Scriptures.

It was near eleven when we retired to our berths in the hope of getting a little sleep before we entered into the rougher part of our journey, but rest and sleep were scarce, the continual coming and going of fresh passengers and the weary night lengthened as the vessel rolled and plunged and we rolled with it.

We eagerly watched the returning light of morning and with unspeakable joy, became conscious of less movement of the ship and longing for fresh air, believed we had time to dress ourselves and go on deck, but proceedings were stopped by the entrance of the steward who took the liberty of rummaging under R's sofa for some of his habiliments and then making a second visit, he peeped in between all the curtains, to the small amusement of the ladies, whilst he demanded their fares.

As soon as he had left the apartment one after another we rolled out of the berths and after many attempts to rise and reach the various articles needed to be able to make an appearance on deck, the feat was accomplished not without much assistance from the stewardess, who said that the sea was as good as land and despite her timely aid we felt that she was a hard hearted woman.

On reaching deck we were delighted at the singular appearance of St Peter Port and the houses of granite interested us much. Castle Cornel was also an object of attraction. It was famously used as a garrison, but at this time only occupied by a few inhabitants, whose business is to startle the town by the firing of the sunrise and sunset guns and to hoist the signals for vessels.

The porters as we landed were vociferous in their entreaties that we would call for them and shouted their numbers which were on plates round their arms, in the hopes of being chosen. Having fixed on one to convey our boxes, we were somewhat surprised with regard to the cheapness of doings in Guernsey, for the demand was of 6^d a head instead of a charge for boxes. It was but a few steps to Marshall's Hotel and here we breakfasted then soon visited the Market which we saw to perfection.

In the open space there were some tents or stalls for biscuits and sweets of every hue, which tempted us at once to become purchasers on behalf of nephews and nieces. Beyond these tables sat a number of women, many in picturesque dresses, with their baskets of vegetables beside them, talking in their 'Guernsey French' to our no small confusion when we attempted to address them, each smiling at the others blunders as we endeavoured to make known our wants and wishes. Then there were others with clean baskets and snow white cloths, containing their nicely washed eggs and delicious butter, coming in shoals to their various seats, all dressed in black bonnets and gowns ready to sell you their goods and give you Doubles into the bargain, six of which half farthings they return for your English shilling.

On the right was an arcade where the French women sat in their little white caps, or you saw the still higher crowns of the Normans, selling their cheap French eggs together with ducks and chickens. And here too it was tempting to stay and look round at the lovely flowers or the beautiful figs and grapes and the splendid pears and apples, and had it not been for the prevalence of CHOLERA I doubt not we should have become good customers. As it was, our brother might still be seen making his lunch of a fig, to the amusement of some unknown lady who reported having seen him enjoying the same.

From thence we will turn to the Fish Market, a covered building with beautiful marble slabs on which lay huge Conger Eels and Red Mullet, and Rock Fish with Turbot, Sand Soles and Sand Eels, Mackerel and Sand Smelts, while upon other tables were abundance of Lobsters and Crabs and Crawfish. Here too was a solitary vegetable stall kept by the Gilliards and of whom we bought roots of the Belladonna, a shilling a dozen. We then stopped to sketch them and also the stall where we purchased "sugarroses".

We then finished our mornings drawing with one of the Guernsey bonnets, all frilled and furbelowed, now worn by the elderly women but which will, I fear with them pass away, as well as the black jackets and black petticoat, which we had just completed, standing behind an old lady, when one of her neighbours to whom she was talking informed her of what we were doing, when she turned round and smiled, and, when showing her the picture, clapped her hands on her knees and chattered away in her unknown tongue to our amusement. We hoped she would have given us her name but on asking for it she replied "Na, Na".

That afternoon we spent visiting the lovely bays of Moulin Huett and Petit Bob, driving through wild passes and across little brooks whose clear streams now and then intercepted our way, luxuriant as they were with watercress and the blue flowers of Brooklime. Here and there a goat was to be seen nibbling the short grass, half hid behind the Furze and Bracken or standing boldly out on a projecting rock.

One of our party, coveting some ferns that were growing on the banks of the lane leading to the Petit Bob and having no tool wherewith to uproot them, we agreed to enter a cottage which was close at hand and see if some implement could be had for the purpose. We forthwith assailed the door with a rap which was speedily answered by an old man who gave us a hearty welcome and with whom we chatted for some time. A French tract lying on the table caused some remarks on reading and his shelves of books were noticed, "Ah" said the old man "but this is my best book", reaching down a large French Bible, the family Bible of many generations. But it was for its contents that it was held in reverence and he told us how he used to sit for hours of an evening reading chapter after chapter feeling, as he went on, that he must still look a little further and a little further, and when at last his wife would suggest that he must have rest he would reluctantly lay it down. Now he had more time for the enjoyment of it as he was past work and this was his only companion, for his wife had been dead three years.

Having obtained the knife which we were in search of, we were about to leave when he prevailed upon us to take some apples which had grown in his own garden.

We returned to our lodgings for tea and after writing home of the adventures of the day we retired to rest, glad indeed that we had a bed to lie on.

The next morning was the Sabbath and we were then first introduced to our friend William Stephens whom we accompanied to Meeting.

We were tired with our walk to the meeting house, short as it was, by its excessive steepness, indeed the streets are nearly all up and down hills, the cart horses which are used for town work are rough shod that they may keep a better footing; it is rare to see a good horse in Guernsey, they are all small and among the `ill favoured and lean fleshed`.

After meeting we took a walk along the esplanade and towards the Sampsons to which place we had intended going but were stopped by a man who, coming across the road, accosted us in broken English with "Now don't go any further, de Cholera is very hard there, two coffins have been carried out dis morning and the grave digger is just gone up again with his spade. You can do as you please, but I say **don't go,** there's no need, why not go up dere (this he said pointing to a hill near us) you will have a good sight of the islands and as fine a fresh air as anywhere, but don't go to the Sampsons". We accordingly followed his advice and a fine fresh air we had and a lovely view of the islands, Alderney, Herm, Jetho and Sark with Jersey and the coast of France in the distance.

The next morning we received a call from W S advising us not to venture to Herm this rough day and we soon after walked with M A to see the steamer come in and then returned to our inn to pack up our traps, and conveyed them to Mrs Mordaunt's lodgings where we took up our abode during the remainder of our stay in the island and having left our packages we set off for a drive to Moye Point. Leaving the carriage as usual in the road, we scrambled over the slippery hills and clinging to ferns and brambles managed by degrees to attain the desired pinnacle whence we sat truly revelling in delight at the grand and lovely scene before us. It was not till we were warned more than once by our brother, of the stormy cloud which was too dark for us not to have seen long ago, that we left our resting place and hastening back towards the carriage were caught in a drenching shower which wetted us through, in spite of our endeavours to shelter ourselves by huddling together behind a large stone with our umbrella and parasol over our heads whilst the drippings from each ran in streams down shoulders, and when we could no longer sit it we pattered through mire and mess till we got back to the coach, meeting the driver half way with our cloaks but being too wet to enjoy ourselves we determined to visit a cottage nearby.

On opening the door we enquired of the woman if she had a fire, but finding she could not understand English, we addressed her in her own tongue as far as we were able and when once our wants were known she retired to a back room and made us a blazing fire of furze and most assiduously aided us in drying our clothes whilst we chatted and laughed and sketched and made ourselves as happy as with the most pleasant adventure.

Our brother walked on, being directed as far as St Peter du Bois where we hoped to overtake him, but so much wet could not be made to evaporate in a short time and long ere we reached that place he had wandered in search of St Andrews which had been fixed as our next resting place. When we got there `the gentleman had not arrived` and the coachman went back by another road in the hope of meeting him while John, in the meantime, made his appearance, but being still wet he spent an hour or so in bed while his garments underwent a similar roasting to our own.

We were not the only travellers on that dreary day, coach after coach and gig after gig drove into the yard; some like ourselves stayed to dine and while beefsteaks were frying, the visitors sang heartily, laughed at each others' misfortunes as well as their own.

We had this morning refused a polite invitation to tea, thinking our excursion would not be ended in time to make the accepting of it suitable, but being thus driven home by the rain earlier than we intended we stopped in the High Street to enquire if it were allowable to alter our minds and to say that `we come`. Our friends' tea was ended and some might have said `they who will not when they may. When they will they shall have nay`, but the kindness we had already received made us venturesome and we could but ask, and none need desire a kinder welcome than fell to our lot as we entered the living room of William and Amy Stephens. (Yet not in our dripping clothes did we go, for Mrs Maidment and the maid Eliza could tell you that the gentleman and ladies had turned their boxes literally inside out and scattering their contents in every direction but into the drawers, their proper place, while stockings were hunted for, dresses and shoes and the maid had to find what ourselves could not see, in our haste to return to our friends).

Our first occupation next morning was enquiring for letters as the steamer from England had arrived about eight and we then turned our steps to the market where, while John and Rebecca were purchasing some of the tempting provisions, I ventured to sketch. The first object I chose for my pencil was a French woman with a high white cap which attracted my fancy but as soon as she saw me at work she walked off and would not sit down till I ended my drawing. I then went up to her telling her what I had done and that I had sketched many others in the market but she still looked solemnly grave as she told me in her patois (which I could not understand without an interpreter) that some years ago a gentleman would have drawn her that he might take her picture to England but she would not allow it even though her daughter much wished it. However we parted friends when we later purchased some eggs at her stall.

Then her opposite neighbour, a Guernsey woman who had been our interpreter sat herself down saying "Now you must draw me, Miss", so having sketched her with her baskets of fruit and the scales and stand of flowers, I asked for her name which she readily gave me as Mary Matry, saying with a nod of her head "there, now you will talk of me when you get to England, if I went there I should like to take drawings of your people".

Next day we took a carriage and horses to Rocquaine Bay, where we strolled along the beach listening to the scream of some small sea birds or startled at the firing of guns from the militia in the distance who were levelling their fire arms at a target out at sea. We then turned inland passing by various churches and schools and watching the beautiful cows in the meadows as they walked the few paces allowed them, demolishing their allotted portion of grass till the farmer thought right to re-tether his kine in a more flourishing spot. This is done two or three times a day, the fields by this means being so much less trodden down can maintain a greater number of cattle which in this island, where farms are so small, is a great advantage. Yet this method of tethering is not without trouble as when storms come on in the night the farmer has to rise and put his cows under shelter. The cows yield most excellent milk and the butter is extremely good. It here seems the custom to milk them three times a day. We were also informed that those cows which were likely to give the best milk might be known by a yellow spot in their ear and a similar ring on the tip of their tail.

We next drove to the Royal Oak. Here we met our brother John and were introduced to the Alexanders. Our Aunt Mary was at work beating the batter for pancakes, nearby stood her sister, the grandmother Rachel who was pouring jar after jar of rich cream into the churn, whilst their son Hillary, with a frying pan in one hand and a fork in the other, zealously cooking the pancakes.

Two little grandchildren stood in the doorway while their old grandfather, almost bent double with age and leaning on his stick, walked past the window on his way to the pigs. Soon entered another of his sons, to whom we were introduced by Aunt Mary, as one of kindred name and we were welcomed with a smile that bespoke at once of goodwill.

We expressed our astonishment that so many generations should dwell under the same roof but Hillary replied that they did not all "stop here", he and his family stopped in one house while his brother with his wife and little ones stopped in another, but they all worked together, one minds the milk and another the farm, while the old father minded the pigs.

We lingered long in the kitchen watching the proceedings and amused by the chatter of English and French which were mixed up together like the milk and the eggs for the batter, to the edification of all. Then we all went upstairs and followed the pancakes, of which we partook in great earnest as we added the sugar and cream, yet soon found them too rich to eat many!. Tea ended, we went downstairs and said goodbye to our friends - "bonsoir" and rejoined our coach.

Next day we again visited the market and some of the shops, being tempted into one by the sight of a doll dressed Guernsey fashion with her baskets of vegetables and fowls at her feet, then spent some time among smelling bottles, papercases, baskets and brooches and dolls of all sizes.

Then we walked up the hill and through a narrow pathway running down the sides of the cliff to a sandy beach where we sat down to rest and enjoy the sea breeze until it was time to return to our `home`.

On our way we passed by 'The Divit' where the French women were washing their linen. This sight was new to us. Mary Ann Stevenson talked to Mrs Abram whilst I took a sketch of the washers. This Mrs Abram was

At 'The Divit'

Visit to market stalls, Guernsey

very communicative telling us the names of the people present, Miss Le Gay, Miss Le Few, Mrs Le Fevre, Mrs Abram and Madame. Madame refused to let hers be known on the score of her not being one of the washers, saying "These women wash for me" and we found it was to her each paid their pence for the accommodation of the Divit, that is a penny for their pail and another for their basket, kneeler and hot water for tea. Mrs Abram had known Mary Ann Stevenson since she was `a tiny wee thing` when she used to come with her Mama to market.

While I was drawing, the Sherriff passed along the road, and looking down to see what was going on, told one of the women she should turn her face to me that I might draw her better because she was so pretty. This caused a laugh among them all and each shouted something to him in return, but as all was spoken in French, I could not understand what was said. We were told that he rarely passed them by without a joke.

Now came our last day on Guernsey, while John and Rebecca went to market, I realised that I had not done a sketch of the Stevensons in their drawing room, so as soon as breakfast was over, I spent some hours there, John and Rebecca returning before I had finished. In the afternoon we walked again to a lovely beach.

Next morning our friends accompanied us to the boat, leaving the Pier as we paced the deck of the Despatch.

We are at Home! A pleasant hour passed the distant Isle of Sark and more near ones of Herm and Jetho on the one hand and Alderney on the other, and a wretched sailing from the Caskets to the Needles in spite of pleasant sun and deep blue waters, and a calm passage past the Isle of Wight brought us to Southampton.

There we slept in a saloon carriage to London and there we rose killing bugs and fleas by hosts. We passed by old haunts till once more seated on a train for Ipswich, we had time to think of all the pleasant times that we had had and to look back with thankfulness for many things. Nor can we look upon our stay without hoping that it was not alone of our own will we went, but was part of that way by which **HE** led us, who only ought to rule our going out and coming in.

Goldrood
20/9/1849

Lithographs - were taken from a stone block, which after the design was traced onto it with greasy chalk, was treated with gum and water so that the unchalked parts rejected the ink and made an impression. Prints produced by these impressions varied. Much collected by the Victorians and shown in this Quakers household rather than pictures.

Market Square, Guernsey

Moulin Huet: sandy bay & rocks, Guernsey

Rock de Guel, Guernsey

Guernsey

Market Square, Jersey

Ten Days in the Isle of Wight

Mary Ann was married just after Christmas in 1850 and this journey was taken with her husband Henry Shewell Corder.

We had a lovely morning to start on our journey and proceeded to London with pleasant company, but it rained as we reached the city and heavy showers succeeded each other during the remainder of the day until reaching Southampton from where the clouds dispersed and a day of sunshine cheered us as we stepped into the packet which was there lying off the pier.

Two hours of pleasant sailing brought us to West Cowes where a boatman coming alongside cried out "Anyone for Cowes?" We determined immediately to proceed thither as our wish was to be located as quickly as possible at Shanklin and this section of the town lay more on our way.

We took up our abode at Medina Hotel for the night, preceding next morning at 10 o'clock in an open carriage to Ryde. We had but a peep at Osborne over the high wall but saw nothing of the Queen and Prince Albert who we were informed had arrived there the night before. Half an hour was all we were allocated at Ryde although the sight of the lovely blue sea as we walked towards the pier made us regret we could not stay longer. Our drive was delightfully varied by occasional views of the sea which was especially attractive at Brading. We also passed by the church where Leigh Bickmaid had preached.

On arriving at Shanklin we drove to Williams Hotel a most picturesque cottage embowered in trees. Here we dined, having first secured ourselves lodgings at Mrs Colmits tempting 'Sea Villa', the first house on the beach. It was a charming place, we passed through a little gateway arched over by Tamarisk which formed a perfect bower and entered the door of the house, on through our now parlour windows, which were thrown open as two glass doors. From thence we had a lovely sea view, which that day looked perfect for those who prefer it as I do calm, quiet, soft and silvery; it was at times all but noiseless, though now and then we heard the breeze like the sound of the advancing tide.

Two pounds a week only we were charged for our two rooms, the sight of two splendid Fuschias on either side of the door and the services of the inmates of the house, from the youngest of whom we received the benefit of an occasional hullabaloo. Though rather given to crying he was a droll little fellow though dotingly fond of a seafaring life, his father rarely returning home but he ran onto the shore to meet him, scrambling into the boat and received the oars eagerly, sitting himself down and performing his mimic voyage by the half hour together. His brother and sisters we saw frequently busily employed under the cliffs picking Copperas and not allowed home until the basket was full.

The first afternoon we took a walk along the beach to Luccombe Chine.

Next day I got up to sketch our pretty abode. After breakfast Henry and I set off for a most bewitching walk along the cliffs, adorned with beautiful trees and enlivened with Guernsey cattle and one solitary small white buffalo.

A little further on we were amused at watching a lovely stork as he stood on one leg, the other stretched out behind him, evidently watching some small frog or toad among the nettles. The next morning we had not recovered from the fatigue of our long ramble but we set out for Carisbrooke Castle. A rather uninteresting drive of 15 miles brought us to Newport. Thence we walked to Carisbrooke castle taking also the circuit of its outside walls. We were surprised to have walked about one mile, after which we entered the gateway. Here the owner made us mount some steps on our left hand pointing on the direction of an iron-barred window through which Charles 1st attempted his escape.

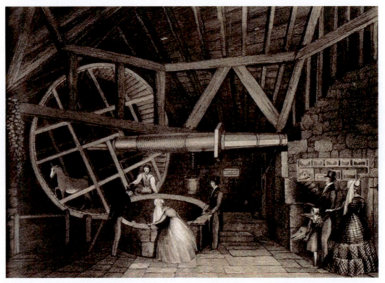

The Mill House at Carisbrooke Castle

We next proceed to the curious well house to watch the clever donkey draw up the bucket (by treading on the wheel) 500 feet deep.

We went home to dinner and then set out to walk to Sandown, where once again we were entertained with the sight of hawks and their young ones which were fluttering and screaming just outside their nest at the very top of the cliff, while the old birds were soaring to and fro at times chasing the crows that flew back and forward as if with some evil design against the nestlings.

We next took a coach and its four horses to Ventnor. We were compelled to ride outside as the inside was full but we didn't regret it, though the wind blew, somewhat boisterously over the hills. We were an hour or so on the beach before taking inside places for Blackgang Chine. The now tremendous wind made us put up more willingly with the narrow coach windows which sadly contracted the glorious sights we would have obtained of majestic rocks towering on our right.

The garden of our inn the Blackgang Chine Hotel, with its various little crevices of rockwork and bold rugged ground and the sea below formed a charming view from our parlour window. We had but a wooden partition between us and a party in the adjoining room so that the endearing epithets and loud shouting to deaf granny were distressing to our nerves!

After breakfast we set out to walk along the clifftops to the village of Miton. Here we were engaged in the most amusing conversation with a Blackgandite. Commencing with the peaceable topic of potatoes and wheat till an allusion to foreign wheat indicated a spirited confab on that warlike spirit, now aroused in foreign countries. Then came the surmise that all our present troubles were owing to the bye past war when 'Blucher came in under French colours' and so enabled the English to win the game, and when the Queen (I suppose the **then** reigning Sovereign was meant) had to borrow so much money off private individuals that she now has to tax her subjects to pay off the interest on the debts.

He then related an instance of a squire near Miton of whom so much was borrowed that ever after he tried to make people believe he had no money and it was hard to get him to pay his debts, yet when he died he had a 'big box almost full of sovereigns and a two gallon jar beside!'

After dinner we set off in high spirits to the highest part of the island, St Catherine's Down. H was in raptures and set off at great speed and I followed him reclining full length on the soft Down, with a most glorious view all around of dazzling views of green hills, blue sky, snowy white and a silvery sea.

We descended at last past the cliff to which quarrymen had directed us and found several small Ammonites and Corals.

Next morning we left Blackgang and drove on to Freshwater Bay, taking up our abode at Albion Hotel from where we walked to the Needles Lighthouse. On May 6th we walked to Alum Bay. On returning to the inn we set-to to make a parcel of our specimens. I broke up a few hard pieces of rock, in which there were many crushed shells and a little coral. These were the only fossils we found from Alum Bay, the name of this bay is derived from little pieces of Alum which are found in the clay of the cliffs.

Albion Hotel, Freshwater Bay

Next we took the 6 o'clock steamer to Lymington and took a walk along the shore to Coleswell Bay, collecting fossil shells - (another little bunch of an atifa) to add to my collection, There we came upon a group of men at work laying the foundations of a new fort which being nearly opposite Hurst Castle was expected to be of great service should an enemy attempt to come between the island and the mainland, as there the firing from each fort would almost preclude the possibility of any vessel passing through unhurt. Hurst Castle is very singularly placed at the point of a very narrow strip of land which stretches a mile into the sea.

On the 2nd day we took a carriage to Brockenhurst and Lyndhurst. After ordering dinner at the inn we drove to Stoney Cross where we walked into the forest to see the stone erected to the memory of William Rufus who was killed there by an arrow which shot him while hunting.

Finally we took a carriage to Beaulieu Station and thence to London a delightful railway ride. Our next resting place was Chelmsford where we finished our months holiday by a pleasant fortnight at Reeds Farm enjoying the company of our relations, with the country life extending to rambles over the harvest fields and gardens and village greens looking into cottages and churches, lingering awhile at the church at Writtle to take a sketch with which I finish my pleasant remembrances.

On the Isle of Wight

Rebecca & Mary Ann at Scarborough

Now for our long talked of holiday in South Shields

(Dark and dismal town of Shields - August 1894)

(Mary Ann and her husband Henry Shewell Corder set out on this journey to visit relations in Shields and to visit Scotland).

Before we get encompassed in the gloom let us take a peep at a few pleasant things by the way. Passing Newmarket we were interested in catching a glimpse of the Devil's Dyke as it is called, being an embankment of seven miles in length in a straight line and raised it is believed in the time of the Mercians.

We proceeded to Huntingdon in a carriage with three postilians for the first, second and third passengers and we were drawn four miles by a horse, the driver sitting on the carriage roof his legs dangling down before our window. Having to wait some time in Huntingdon, we walked down by the river and on the bank I took a sketch of the opposite side.

From here we went to visit our Corder cousins in Kempton. On our way we noticed many acres of onions in fields and gardens, making good profit and growing them both for root and seed. Cucumbers are usually grown in great quantities and sent North, but this year they have all failed, being a great loss to the people of Sandy. Lodging at the Railway Hotel, Peterborough, we visited next morning the Cathedral and then went on our way to York where we exchanged a few hurried words with our three nephews who had escaped from Bootham School to meet us.

We then resumed our seat and were much amused by a conversation with a fellow passenger and his pretence of learning. Many times reminding us while pointing to the fields of corn on either side, that "the prospects are an aspect of pleasantness" and then "The country here was more salubrious and not so dormant as Knaresborough", - and during the thunderstorms which followed, assured us that "these things rarified the air".

From Gateshead station, standing soaking on the platform, grumbling for want of shelter, that we were cold there is no doubt and wrapping ourselves in our plaids and stamping our feet we frowned and laughed and scolded and chattered in turn. A train arrived from Newcastle and we dawdled on to South Shields. Here our brother Frederick meets us and conducted us through the dark unknown to his own bright and comfortable dwelling.

Here we were greeted by our sister Jane whilst Aunt Mary, loving as ever made things more homish still.

Next morning there was a girl at the door calling "Caller Herrings", which we were meant to buy. Next we went by steamer up the Tyne to Newcastle calling on James and Mary Watson and their herd of children.

Then we went on our excursion to Whitby where we wandered on the beach searching for sea anemones and shellfish to carry home.

Next day we went by train to Carlisle where we just had time to see round Slater's Biscuit Factory, then took a train to Beatock having entered Scotland at the far famed Gretna, where a lady in the same carriage said "La, what is this Gretna?"

We drove beside Moffat Water which flows into the Irish Sea. We stopped at a wayside house near the Lock of Lowes where we dined off chops and bacon and when we queried "How much to pay?" we were told "Sure you know as well as I, t'will be two shillings for yourselves and the same for the food".

Each room in the house seemed to be both a bedroom and a dining room for travellers, sometimes occupied by two parties at the same time. We therefore had no wish to take up our abode there, although it all looked very clean and comfortable.

Next was Selkirk, which looked a rubbishy place after Moffat and we had to get in at the inn where a drunken man met us at the door, which gave us rather a disgust of the place. But the inn was very full but we had a first rate room for us to sleep in, though the windows were propped up by a brick, yet the people did their best to make us comfortable. The sitting room was good with a cheerful fire and we enjoyed our evening reading 'Sunny Memories'

At Galashiels we splashed through the rain to Watson's Warehouse to purchase plaids but nothing took our fancy. So we had to wait at the station for the next train. We did not feel in a very bright frame of mind and queried whether it would be best to take the first train home and go to bed for a week! So much for a lark! The best thing here was a purchase of three pen'oth of biscuits, served with a gigantic cup of tea with a plentiful accompaniment of bread and butter which might be had for the asking, only cakes expected to be paid for.

At Kelso we went by omnibus to Cross Keys to a comfortable inn and at the Post Office called in and collected a letter from Rebecca. We sat by the lovely River Tweed and look at the residences here and the seats and gardens placed at the water's edge.

Soon after 9.00am we set off in a dog cart for Wooller, as our drive did not lay close under the Cheviot Hills, they did not look as high as I had expected, neither were they all purple with heather but cut out into squares and triangles with stone walls and hedges. Our carriage came to a third gate and our driver asked if we were to pay for that too - "Ah no, those were in Scotland and this is in England". "In England." I said to myself, "Come all this way to be among Scotch hills and all at the very least to be in the mysterious land that is between England and Scotland, as if I was in Suffolk, this was too great a shock!"

However we left Wooller cottage after ordering dinner and proceeded to find hills for a climb. We had not gone far before came a shower of rain, we had no plaid nor umbrella and so sat ourselves by the nettles by the road.

A good view of the Cheviots and Hambledon and Flodden where the Earl of Northumberland and his son Hotspur defeated the Scots and took the Earl of Douglas prisoner.

Next we went for a long walk to Brizby. We looked along the coast to the mouth of the Tweed, Holy Island, Bamborough Castle, North Sunderland, Alnmouth and Workmouth, we refreshed ourselves by a draft of clean water from the 'Lady Well'. The road took us past the castle gateway and a noble and ancient building but as the Duke of Northumberland had just arrived, no visitors were allowed to see over it.

Among the towers and battlements were many figures of the size of life in various positions, attitudes and attired which have a peculiar effect but whether this is in poor taste I leave to decide by more competent judges.

In making our way towards the entrance we saw by the roadside a stone erected to mark the spot where in 1174 William the Lion, King of Scotland was taken prisoner whilst besieging the castle.

By this time we looked at our Bradshaw and realised we only had six minutes to get to the train. Not a scrap of lunch, I scampered upstairs to get the luggage, Henry paid the bill, we threw the key out of the window and reached the station in time. We found a few crumbs of biscuit in our bag and had a delicious drink of water.

Passing through many stations we reached Beal to try to get a boat to Holy Island. A man who owned a little boat promised to come for us and would take us across in the evening.

There was no shop in the village. We asked at a cottage to try and purchase some food but the only one we found answered us gruffly and we did not apply to her to supply our wants. At last we came to a pump but though we pumped it was dry. At last we gathered a few hips and haws, one was ripe and the others naught but stone, so we returned to the shore.

We had not been long before a gentleman drove down in his gig. The sun was setting and the little cart appeared and tumbled our luggage into his cart. Then our gentleman appeared and took us across to Lindisfarne. The first inn had no room for us but our gentleman accompanied us to another inn, close by the Abbey ruins, where we were comfortably accommodated and at 8.00pm we partook of boiled ham and bread and butter! We had plated teaspoons and two moulded candles instead of leaded spoons and rush lights, so we had not come to such an outlandish place as I had anticipated.

When morning came, we visited the ruins of the Abbey which are interesting because from their association with the early history of Christianity in Britain and largely as the residents of St Cuthbert's. Having inspected these ruins we toiled across to the other side of the island, where we saw one of the sources of wealth by burning lime, which is said to be of a very special quality and is conveyed by train to the haven. We also visited a fine salmon net which the fishermen were repairing but the quantity caught of this fish is trifling, compared with that of herring, which forms an important item in their affairs and we had evidence in the quantity of barrels filled and filling with this useful food. The other half of the island is cultivated and has good fields of corn, turnips and potatoes and in the gardens we saw gooseberry bushes as well as a variety of course trees but these were not abundant.

We now returned back to Rodericks 12.00 lunch or more properly dinner, for our liberal host had provided salmon trout, lamb chops and apple pudding.

The boat was now ready to take us across to Bamborough Sands and the boatman with his daughter, who managed the oar well, soon rowed us round across the channel which at this point is twenty foot deep at low tide and now looked like a beautiful crystal green. A coach was waiting our arrival and backed into the water to meet the boat so we jumped in and he was soon pulling us on those beautiful sands where shells should have been sought instead of on Holy Island. We had to travel inland to reach the village of Banborough, and then having ordered tea we sallied forth to walk on the seashore, the tide was coming in with splendid breakers and pounding towards the shore. We then mounted over the sands onto the castle which is very interesting though much of it has been rebuilt of late years. It stands on a bold rock 150 feet high and before the invention of cannon must have been a very strong fortress and was used as such in early times. It is now used in different ways having been left in trust by Lord Crewe, Bishop of Durham with other properties.

Our journey back from Shields was long and tedious. From Bamborough we journeyed slowly to Newcastle and hence by train to London, then home to Chelmsford. This had been a strange experience with pleasant memories of family and friends visited, long periods of near starvation only assuaged sips of cold water and comforted with thoughts of our comfortable little home at Chiltern Cottage which awaited us.

At Loch Katrine

Returning from London

At home in Meadow Cottage

Marianne Corder - A few memories of a long life

Marianne was born on February 23rd, 1857 and died aged 90 in 1947. Her brother Harry was two years older. When she was 78 she was persuaded to write some of her memories. (She was born with a dislocated hip and was a cripple all her life.)

Henry & Marianne (nicknamed Polly)

I, Marianne Corder, may be said to have begun my existence as a 'Suffolk Dumpling' though later became an 'Essex Calf', born at our house in Tavern Street, Ipswich to which I always felt a great affection. My great Uncle Edward Corder, the head of the firm of which my Father (Henry Shewell Corder) was partner.

I think, my earliest remembrance, just feeling that he took me into his office, and perhaps there were little apples to tempt his great niece. I still have a bag on which he printed 'Polly' and was told that was a sample of my first sewing; it was made for a bunch of grapes in his vinery, vine still bearing in 1936.

As we moved to Fyfield in Essex when I was two or three years old I cannot say more of Ipswich in my early days, though my many visits there in later years, always gave me pleasure.

The next, perhaps 3 or 4 years were spent at Fyfield at the farm Uncle Octavius Corder and Aunt Margaret owned. Soon after our arrival there Harry and I got whooping cough, and I fear passed it on to our little cousin Mary Margaret. Grandpa (her Father) took us to Bexhill to get strong again. I can remember nothing of the visit except sinking in a quicksand from which my Father happily rescued me.

Uncle Octavius was a great singer and used to delight us with his songs. 'I'd rather go to Jericho, than a doctor's boy I'd be' or 'You shall mind the dairy while I shall guide the plough' but my favourite was 'T'is the song the sigh of the weary, hard times, hard times, come again no more' (etc.)

and after nearly **seventy** years great was my delight on hearing this on the radio.

The only time I ever tasted beer was when Uncle Octavius gave me some bitter beer and soda in a little silver mug! I quite enjoyed it!

The little village children brought us lovely bunches of spring flowers on May Day – also I have distant memories of kindly people. Mrs Eves who always gave us a welcome and let a greedy little girl find her way to the sideboard for lumps of sugar.

Mrs Algar, Rev. Gibson and others – we attended the church there as the nearest meeting of Friends (Quakers) was eight miles away.

After some years, we took a farm at Writtle named 'Rollestones' and my parents remained there for twenty or more years I think. Certainly happy carefree years. My walks with 'Papa' in the harvest fields and meads were one of my chief delights, in early years, sometimes visiting the cottagers, and they **were** poor in those days and I must needs always ask my Mother for something to take them, as I could not bear to go empty handed - if an egg was the gift I had to go without one for breakfast, but must say that 'Mama' always gave me half hers!

Sometimes it was the cottagers who were the givers, and I well remember sitting on a little stool while the kind woman toasted and buttered a slice of bread for me - never was toast so good.

Sometimes when the corn was cleared from the harvest fields we would go and help the gleaners to pick all we could for our favourites among them, also sometimes we drove the donkey cart to the field with buns, ripe or baked apples and rice pudding perhaps for the gleaners lunch. Then they more than rewarded us with little home - made loaves, made from the gleaned corn - so sweet and good.

A lady living at a lovely house named 'Hylands' was Mrs Pryor the wife of our landlord and she kindly gave me a pair of lovely white rabbits, with dark ears and pink eyes.

Her little daughter had some and spared a pair for me. How well I remember falling on the polished marble hall and Mrs Pryor picking me up under her arm, so I cannot have been very old then. These bunnies had a family later on, but through want of proper care only one survived. I was allowed to keep them until my school days commenced, though our old gardener, King, had so much trouble with them, cleaning the cage etc., that he said it was quite time they were put in a 'dough cage', meaning a pie! He was a quaint man and was too proud ever to ask a favour, if he wanted vegetables saved he would write on them "please save me" or "please do not eat me" and when he needed a new shoe cleaning brush, he would hang a ticket on the old one "please I'm worn out".

Of course my brother Harry and I were very fond of playing in the near-by gravel pit, or in the barns where the men thrashed out the corn with flails, and there was great delight when the engine came to thresh, the engine driver being a great favourite of ours.

How well I remember a young deer fleeing from the huntsmen and taking refuge with us - Oh! So pitiful to see its panting and its beautiful eyes begging us to be merciful. We longed to hide it in one of the attics but it had to remain in the calves pen until the huntsmen discovered its whereabouts, then it was removed to be chased another day! How we hated huntsmen and all their works. Though I do remember once that they had the 'meet' at our farm and I handed out sandwiches and wine. That was before we all signed the pledge (for the sake of example to others) at a meeting in our large kitchen.

Our landlord always sent us a barrel of ale at Christmas but when our pledge was taken we had to refuse his well meant gift. (He was a brewer, so naturally beer was a usual gift to him), after that he sent a barrel of apples, which, as we had a large orchard was not quite appropriate! He also sent us grouse when in Scotland for the sport. Once I remember they were so 'high' that our maids refused to prepare them, but Uncle Edward Corder of Reeds Farm, gladly accepted them! My dear old grandmother lived at Reeds earlier on, and we always spent Christmas Day with her. She had a lovely dairy, and sweet smelling store cupboard. I remember reading a psalm to her when she was ill in bed, but I think my dearest memory was of her sweet old face with fair curls, showing in her black satin 'Quaker' bonnet as her son drove her to meeting. Her presents to her children and grandchildren were florins or half crowns wrapped in silver paper and handed round at dessert on a green vine leaved dish, matching all the other dessert set at Christmas time.

In one of my walks with my Father he reproved a school boy for trespassing and received an amusing letter of apology later on which ended, "give my love to the little angel at your side who smiled so sweetly at me, Yours penitently ....". Very amusing no doubt, but when my parents read it aloud to their friends the Christys, I vanished under the table to hide my blushes!

Another visitor whose remarks have always remained in my memory, was the respected old Friend Isaac Brown. He called me to him and asked me "where is thy soul dear?" and on patting my pinafore, he laughed so much that I spent all the rest of the day in the tool shed, and avoided him. I wonder if **he** could have told **me** where his soul was!

When ten years old I went to Miss Hick's school as a weekly boarder and was very happy there, especially under Miss Prissie Hick's care. She was very kind always and once when her sister sent me to bed without any tea, she brought me up some sponge cake and milk. Our drilling and drawing masters were my favourites, but with the French teacher I was not at all a success. He told me I was "like a fortress without a gun" etc. and no doubt he had reason for such expressions, as I was a great failure with that language. The only great strictness I remember in my three years at that school was when one of us bought a mask on the 5th of November, it was immediately put on the fire!

My Father always drove in from Writtle to take me home on Saturday and my great delight was to be allowed to drive, this as a rule I managed in safety, though once the reins got crossed so that we drove into a ditch, happily not a deep one. We were very happy at school there but poor Prissie Hicks had to tell me off sometimes. She would say "I knew a little maiden once and Marianne was her name and many a naughty thing she did I tell it to her shame," but we were always good friends.

As we lived at Writtle, a quiet little village then (but became an important place as the first Headquarters of 2LO) we had three miles to walk, or drive, to meeting on Sunday. The horse was only taken out in the morning, so it entailed, to me, a tiring journey (because she was lame) in the afternoons or evenings, through fields of waving corn or the ramble by the brook and over the wooden bridge in the park, then called Admiral's Park.

On Sunday evenings we listened (or slept through!) one of Spurgeon's sermons, which was my Father's weekly reading, then to conclude the day we sang, perhaps not very tunefully but with enjoyment, many well known hymns. One was my favourite 'The Lord's my Shepherd'.

I remember well, having measles, and my Mother was away from home. During the night troublous "nightmares" came to me and I shrieked out in fear. When my Father appeared and tried to comfort me all I could say was – "You will never forgive me, I've eaten one of your lambs and the skin's hanging up in the hall". Of course he said it didn't matter, I might eat them all! The next dream was the same, but this time it was a sheep which I had devoured, and left the skin in the hall. The third time my appetite was evidently increasing and I had managed to eat a bullock, but every time my cry was "You will never forgive me".

The next morning they found me all over measles "and that's that!"

Our maids once took Harry and me to tea at the cottage where the parents of one lived, I think we went in a donkey cart, and remember having redcurrant wine given to us, also hearing of the poor diet of the days of low wages when 'swedes' were the principal food, I took it to mean 'sweets' and quite envied them, and they had 'blackbread' which was a treat.

Once I stayed at Writtle Park with Eliza Marriage and she later took me to Tunbridge Wells with her and her little daughter. How I enjoyed spending pennies she gave me, and walking on the Pantiles. We stayed at Calvary Crescent and there was an Italian 'Count' next door, at least we were told so, and I remember my great interest in seeing him giving a gold coin to an Italian organ grinder.

I remember the large rocks in a field at Tunbridge Wells 'Toad Rock'.

The longest drive I ever remember was from Chelmsford to Ipswich. My Father drove and we reached Colchester in time for breakfast, which we had at Uncle Joseph Shewell's home. He was my great uncle, and a well known preacher in the "Society of Friends".

I think that was the occasion when we saw pineapples growing in the pinery belonging to Corder Catchpool's grandfather. We then drove on to Ipswich.

Another early visit with my parents was to Norwich where Uncle Octavius had taken a chemist's shop. We dined one day with Henry (or Josiah) Brown. We had oyster sauce with the fowl at dinner and my mother found a pearl in hers.

We visited relations in Bedfordshire, Great Aunt How. Great Aunt Maria Thorp at Dunstable, who gave me a bright coloured straw basket made there. Uncle Thomas, and his wife, we also visited, and his daughter Mary who later married a Mr Downing and had a daughter Dorothy. Earlier on, perhaps, was a visit to Aldbourough where my cousin Constance and Alice Alexander and I had the pleasure of seeing and nursing triplets, two boys and a girl belonging to a sailor's wife. (I think I still have the photographs of them).

Dorothy Downing, mentioned just previously, was of a rather adventurous nature and got into great trouble for joining with some other children in a 'raid' on their neighbours 'taking', without leave, a barrow and then eggs and various things which they went round trying to sell. Police got hold of her as the ring-leader and she was sent to a reformatory, there were long descriptions of the 'raid' in the Daily papers (this perhaps in the 1930s).

Some visits to London I remember, going to the British Museum, which I thought very dull, and got woefully tired.

Kew Gardens were more to my taste, and I remember seeing the Victoria water lilies. We climbed the monument, visited St Pauls and the whispering gallery there. Also once to the Crystal Palace where Blondin went up a spiral stair on a great ball.

We often were kindly entertained at the house 'Westfield' belonging to Caroline Marriage of Chelmsford. I seem to call to mind many breakages that I was guilty of; broke a nice iron table by sitting on it and swinging round, also a lovely green and gold cream jug when the kind old Quaker lady allowed me to pour out tea.

An early recollection of our election was when I was spending the day there, and waved a little yellow card out to the butcher boy in blue saying – "Yellow for ever down with the blue".

Uncle Maw's house at Needham Market was another delightful place to visit, a donkey to ride when Uncle rattled his stick in his top hat to make it hurry its paces.

The Maze to puzzle us, and the aviary with lovely silver or gold pheasants etc. and a large pond where Cousin Tom's wonderful little steam boat was a pleasure.

Uncle Frederick Alexander also entertained my parents and self and drove us over to see 'Burstall Hall' an old family home. We also visited an old lady of 107 who sang to us. The only time I have met a centenarian, **she** said she was 111 but I am not sure!

When thirteen years old I was sent to Lewes School, kept by Mary and Catherine Trusted and Rachael Special. There were only twenty-six boarders, several other girls went from Chelmsford and the Father of one or another family saw us off in London. Our favourite lunch, before starting, was oxtail soup or something easy to swallow in our very weeping condition. We did not go off to school so cheerfully as children do in the present day, and I well remember David Christy insisting on our having roast beef rather than soup and how hard it was to get the red meat down without choking!

Some girls write very happily of their time at Lewes, but it was often detested by me, and many a time after I left school I would dream of it and wake to find my pillow wet with tears. Doubtless it was that I was not a favourite with either teachers or scholars, and the former were often unduly strict and gave me punishments that to this day I feel were unjust and unfair. Rachel Special was more thoughtful for me and often got me excused some of the long walks which tried my lame leg very much, especially when there were the great chalks hills and downs to climb. I supposed they little guessed how weary I became. Still I can remember some delightful walks in the Spring and the pleasure of finding wild flowers. Then excursions by brake to various places of interest, such as Arundel, Pevensey, Eastbourne etc. Brighton we also visited, at the time of the British Association Meeting, and I remember hearing the blind Professor Fawcett speak there.

Another visit was with Mr & Mrs David Christy who took some of us out in a boat. Never should I want to go through such an experience again.

My cousin Louis Alexander, when staying at Tunbridge Wells, asked me over there from Lewes and that was a great pleasure.

The great event of the year was the carnival on Guy Fawkes Day, when we were allowed to look from the bedroom windows upon the procession of people in every conceivable dress, quantities of fireworks and blazing tar barrels. Lewes is still, I believe, one of the most noted places for such a display.

There were no prizes given in the school but I was very pleased one year to gain a prize for freehand drawing and a certificate for model drawing, all the schools had competed, and the Earl of Chichester presented the prizes. Mine was a paintbox.

There were no bathrooms in the school house and I was greatly surprised the first time some of us were taken out in the evening to the Public Baths. There was also a nice open-air bath which many enjoyed but as I had never been taught to swim, I did not find great pleasure in my baths.

Kind Friends at Lewes sometimes asked us out to tea, and to walk round their beautiful gardens in the summer.

On leaving school at the age of sixteen I went to my happy home at 'Rollestons', Writtle, and can picture many a drive and pleasant outing, with or without visitors. When friends stayed with us, our usual drive for them was to Danbury, or through the Grace's walk. Various cousins stayed with us, those from Norwich, Uncle Octavius' family, Robin and May Spence, 'Attie' and Annie Corder.

They were all about the age of my brother and self and we had rare times climbing the stacks, and listening to the chorus of voices as one or another sang to us. May Spence had a sweet voice for the north-country songs, and 'Attie' and Annie were very tuneful and musical and their various songs are in my memory still. Many a pleasant time we had on the ice in the winter time, though skating was not an accomplishment I could shine in. My lameness was a drawback but I loved trying to get about however hopeless it was. The lake at Hylands Park was a delight, also the nice parties we were invited to join in at Broomfield Hall, where bonfires were lighted round the pond, then after skating, to gather round the hospitable table of Mr & Mrs Impey.

We enjoyed going to 'Book Meetings' and 'Essay Meetings', nothing more exciting came our way, and we were always content with simple pleasures.

Ten or more of the young Friends of the meeting at Chelmsford started what we called 'The Happy Thought Club'. This continued in being for several years, and the whole party, sometimes with extra visitors, started gaily forth in a brake and pair for Epping Forest, or on the Laindon Hills; and later the great idea was to write accounts of adventures in poetry or prose. We also went to Epping Forest as a family party only, and once were caught in a great rain storm. After sheltering under the beech trees for some time, we were suddenly deluged, and had a fine time getting to the station with the water squelching in our boots.

Flower shows at the various mansions and estates round about Chelmsford were another delight – any at Hylands especially were enjoyable.

When staying with Bessie Marriage at the Lodge, I remember an early morning before breakfast, drive up to Galleywood Common, and had a climb up the tower of the New Church which was then in the course of erection.

Another time a party of young people climbed up the belfry of Writtle church while the ringers were practising on the peal of bells.

Mary Spence, who was the same age as I, visited with me at Ipswich. Uncle Frederick Corder had a nice house, very ancient, on St. Margaret's Green. The well known family of Cobbolds had lived there years before and their servant Margaret Catchpole was a well known character. Mr J Cobbold wrote the history of her life, she was in love with some wild fellow and got mixed up with some smugglers. She was once put down the well in the gardens of St. Margaret's House.

May and I visited Norwich and stayed with Uncle Octavius and Aunt Margaret. Our visit was enlivened by a day on the Norfolk Broads, by kind invitation of a curate, Rev W Cant who had a yacht for our day's excursion, he also presented us with hymn books, pictures, sweets etc.

and asked for our photographs in return – even offered to **pay** for mine and got it!

Some very pleasant visits were paid to our relations in the north. Uncle John Spence of North Shields was a great favourite, and many a pleasant time I can remember there. Once at a display of life saving apparatus, when the 'Breeches Buoy' was worked from the cliff to the end of the pier, I was foolish enough to refuse the offer of a trial trip. Uncle Spence, also Uncle Frank Corder, were both great at helping the lifeboat crews. Uncle John Spence also took my father and myself down a coal mine. We first had some distance to go on the coal train and I sat on a heap of coals on the tender, the driver having the courtesy to offer his coat for me to sit on. Then at the mine we entered the cage and down we went feeling as though we were fast going **up** instead of **down**. I never forgot the politeness shown by the north-country people, porters and miners and so on.

In the narrow workings of the mine with the little coal trucks whizzing past, they would call out "Take care honey, it's vie grazy". We had sometimes to bend double in the lower workings, some had candles and some Davy lamps to light us. The men were singing and seemed cheerful, but I am sure if we had much experience of living in such darkness, and often unable to stand upright, we should have far more sympathy for our brothers, the miners.

Another pleasant visit was to Sunderland to stay with Uncle Alexander Corder and his five lively sons. He was always most kind, and I think it was he who took us on a pleasant excursion to Ainwick Castle.

We sometimes crossed in the ferry boat from Sunderland to Shields and great was my disappointment not to meet with the faithful sheep dog "wandering Willie" which went back and forth daily on the boat in hope of finding his shepherd master whom he had lost by accident years before.

In 1875 or 1876 I believe it was, I paid my first visit to Ireland, staying with H J and A Allen at 'Ferndene', near Dublin. We took the night sail and it was quite a disagreeable experience for me, the going on board in the darkness, and it was my first boat trip. During my stay there I saw some of the beautiful scenery surrounding Dublin, both inland and by the sea. Visited Catholic Cathedrals for the first time, and was able to attend the meeting of Moody and Sankey once or more. One of Sankey's favourite hymns was 'there were ninety and nine that safely lay' etc etc, and the lines in some of those verses must have taken hold on the mind of some young shopman, as I remember that, when he was serving us with gloves, all his sentences were mixed with the lines "I go to the desert to find my sheep". Perhaps he preached a sermon without being aware of it!

My brother came over and also visited at Ferdene and then escorted us home, he insisted on my staying on deck on the return voyage and as it was a day trip, it turned out to be quite enjoyable.

We visited Chester together, the Cathedral and City walls, and the lovely quaint covered shops. One visit that was even earlier, when I had just left school (about 1873) was to Hunstanton, where Aunt R B A and I stayed with Uncle Octavius and his family.

Curiously enough in the adjoining lodgings were the Penrose family, the sister was one of my school friends. There were several of her brothers there. One was later on the well-known artist J Doyle Penrose who painted the Quaker picture 'The Presence in the Midst', 'the Quaker Wedding' and others.

We met and became acquainted with other interesting people and visited at some quaint old fashioned cottage where the old gentleman gave us tea in old blue china service, with tiny mouthfuls of bread and butter, to match the little plates, and not our seaside appetites!

I enjoyed visiting the lighthouse etc. My cousin Mary and I tried an early morning bathe, but as neither of us could swim we ran quite a risk wading out as far as we could, and had quite a difficulty to get back as the tide was coming in.

There are various incidents which I have omitted, the remembrance of the day of festivity when King Edward and Queen Alexandra (then Prince and Princess of Wales) were married. Then a bazaar held in the village school room where a kind old Friend CM, mentioned previously, gave me 10/- to spend. I was greatly tempted by a lovely doll, which would have taken all the money, and I was unwise enough to spend on smaller purchases which were not lasting.

My Father, Mother and Aunt were so busy at the stalls of the bazaar and not able to return to our home to our 1 o'clock dinner so my brother and I finished up their share of the sausages as well as our own, much to the chagrin of our elders when they returned faint and hungry!

After leaving school I was considered of an age to go up to Yearly Meeting (Quaker Y M) with my Mother and we stayed at an hotel in Bloomsbury, our breakfast usually consisted of 'am and heggs' or 'heggs and am' as far as I remember there was not much variety.

That must have been a time when Moody and Sankey were preaching and singing to crowded meetings in London and was the only time I entered a theatre when we heard them both - (or was it the Agricultural Hall, Islington).

After that we usually had a day or two (Quaker) yearly Meeting and some of the great crowds in our large Meeting House made quite an impression on me.

Around this time I was bridesmaid at the wedding of my cousin Hettie Alexander to J Fyfe Stewart - this took place at Ipswich. I may be the only survivor of that occasion.

Aunt Maria Corder kindly entertained me and drove me up to see the old home of Goldrood, where my mother lived before her marriage and it is the only time I have seen it and then only the exterior. It overlooked the River Orwell.

One of my great delights when in London in May were the visits to the Royal Academy. This was an annual pleasure for some years.

A visit to Aunt Lucy How at Aspley Guise in Bedfordshire was and still is one of my most pleasant remembrances. May Spence and I were invited together and stayed with cousins Maria Thorp part of the time. When at Aunt How's, a most charming place with five large fish ponds divided by grass paths and overshadowed with tall trees, I had my one and only experience of fishing, with a rod and hook.

I was very successful and caught eight fish, but the last one was so entangled with the hook that my distress was too great to continue the sport. Aunt had many fine and curious shrubs and trees and her allspice bush was the only one I saw.

Cousin M Thorp took us for an excursion to Woburn Abbey, the seat of the Duke of Bedford and we were allowed to view some part of the place where the statuary was displayed. On our return May and I were amused to hear M Thorp's remarks to Aunt How – "What do you think we saw, dear Aunt!" "I don't know child" (the 'child' must have been about sixty) "Why, Aunt dear we saw a nood figure of the dook". "Thee don't say so child" holding up her hands in horror! The 'nood' figure was simply one of the young Duke in cricket costume! Uncle How had been librarian to the previous Duke, and had left a very interesting library of his own with wonderfully illuminated Bibles or other books.

Once at a large temperance bazaar in London I was invited to sell buttonholes and quite enjoyed the experience. I had painted some illuminated texts for one stall, the Essex stall, and many years after was amazed to see one framed in an Essex rectory and found that it had been purchased at the bazaar. I also was asked to paint texts for the 'Red Cow'

Temperance Hotel in Chelmsford, miserable performances but they still hung there many years later!

My Father gave me the use of a field and the profits of crop, if any, were to come to me. All I can remember in the way of work was learning to plough a furrow or two, but the long dresses worn in those days were not suitable for a 'land girl'.

One of the Friends of Chelmsford Meeting, Philip M riding by on horseback at the time, must have been greatly astonished to see me with the plough.

Driving, as I mentioned previously, was a great pleasure to me, and my menfolk, Father and Brother gave way to me on many occasions. Once when my Brother was driving through Chelmsford and was not paying attention to his duty, a man called out "where are you going to muttonhead". Other sayings return to my memory as people talking of 'Uncerated London News' or 'Consecrated Coconut'. A proud Mother described her infant son as "a Turk, a reg'lar Rooshan". One when calling with a message instead of writing it said "It would be hand to mouth, as the saying is". When an elderly lady was calling on us and tore her dress on the step, her old coachman said "A good thing 'twarnt your best one".

In the late autumn of 1877 I became engaged to Herbert Marriage much to the surprise of my family, and I may add my own, though we had known each other for some years. We had many pleasant times together, one day which stands out in my memory was one we spent together at the Crystal Palace.

In the Spring of 1878 he went with me to Ipswich to be introduced to my many relations in Suffolk. Uncle Fred and Aunt Maria Corder, Uncle Fred Alexander and Aunt Lydia who though a very prim Quakeress had the inspiration to give us heart shaped cakes for our tea!

Needham Market was also visited to see Aunt Rachel Maw, and at Woodbridge we found Aunt Anna Alexander and Agnes ready to give us a warm welcome at Bank House. I was only 21 that Spring, but was intending to marry in the summer, so at the old shop in Tavern Street looked out various garments for my trousseau with the help and guidance of my good Father.

I chose a mauve silk wedding dress, with the absurdly long trains of the period, a pale blue dress likewise with long train edged with white lace, a sensible fawn poplin, a delicate cotton dress, a sealskin jacket, silk cloth ditto. My travelling dress was grey braided and with sleeveless coat to match and a grey hat with ostrich feather, a very neat bonnet for Sunday wear trimmed with cream silk ruchings. Somethings I did not buy wisely or well which has given me regret in later years.

While at Ipswich we attended the evening meeting of Friends and were very much surprised towards the close, when an elderly gentleman came in and after divesting himself of several wraps he all the time sizzling tremendously, then knelt down and prayed very beautifully, prayed for Peace etc then after more sizzling asked if he might be allowed to read a portion of scripture 21st of Ezekiel then preached a splendid sermon, said that Friends ought to be as earnest as their glorious forefathers, that they might be willing to go to Russia and plead with the Tsar for Peace. The scourge of war sent as judgement for wickedness and this country should pray that the impending evil might be averted. This is chiefly extracts from a letter written at the time, April 1878. I believe the speaker was Fitzgerald. Several years later I heard him speak at Woodbridge, on the work and teaching of Moody and Sankey and he then acted most strangely, taking off his shoes and marching back and forth on the platform in his grey socks - also took the hats of other speakers and changed them - no notice was taken of these eccentricities for he was evidently well known and respected.

Herbert and I went up to London to see the opening of parliament by Queen Victoria, and though I cannot claim to having seen **her** I enjoyed seeing the beautiful carriage drawn by cream coloured horses (with cream trappings as far as I remember).

We also went to Hyde Park to see the riders in Rotten Row and we were horrified when one horse ran away with its lady rider. The poor creature reached the park palings and in trying to leap them got impaled, the railing spike caught in its throat, and the lady was thrown and injured. It is a horrid recollection.

About this time, February 23rd, I celebrated my 21st Birthday and had a good many gifts suitable for house furnishing etc. as our wedding was to take place in June. We had a busy time then preparing for the lodging of guests and even the attics had to be turned into bedrooms, and the kitchen, a large old fashioned one, was converted into a refreshment room where the wedding breakfast was served. People were most kind in bringing us flowers so that the room was decorated and one Friend sent most beautiful hothouse flowers which were used for bouquets and a wreath for me, but whether it was becoming or not I shall never know! One of our workmen and his wife pleased me greatly by bringing me a beautifully arranged display of white, blue and pink flowers.

The weather was of the warmest and I found it so when concocting all the delicacies for the Wedding Breakfast and had to keep going down to our cool cellar to get freshened up. We had a large bath down there and got some ice round which to place the jellies, custards, blancmanges etc. Unfortunately, as I heard afterwards, they were forgotten and never appeared at the festive occasion!

I think we had sixty visitors so wonder even now, if all got "a comfortable sufficiency" as some quaint Friend would have expressed it! But there were plenty of meals and picnics at which they came in handy. From time to time relations kept arriving and we had quite a large party to tea that evening. I awoke that morning "with the lark" for once on the day of our wedding to a most perfect cloudless morning, and the first sound I heard was a stealthy footstep on the gravel, on looking out what should I see but our old gardener carefully digging up all the plants in the front beds, which would not flower and replacing them with barrow loads of flowering ones from his own cottage garden, surely that was a kindly deed and I relate it here with gratitude.

When decorated suitably I was driven in to Chelmsford in a carriage with two greys, and accompanied by my parents. The only rice I had thrown at me was on the way to the ceremony by the doctor's little daughter.

As was the custom among Friends in those days the Bride and Groom walked up the meeting together and we were followed by Edward Grey and Bessie Marriage, Henry Corder and Alice O Alexander, Frederick George Marriage and May Spence, Arthur B Corder and Edith Marriage (1937). Four of these have passed away before me (now five 1941).

Several Friends and relations addressed the meeting and we the Bridegroom and Bride repeated the usual and I think beautiful words as follows:-

"In the fear of the Lord, and in the presence of this assembly, I take this my friend...........to be my husband promising through Divine assistance to be unto him a faithful and loving wife, until it may please the Lord by death to separate us."

Thomas K. Catchpool had most kindly executed a beautiful certificate which was signed by numerous people after the meeting was over.

Then we, the happy pair, were driven off and went round by Galleywood Common and so home, first calling in on a bedridden man to give him a flower from my bouquet and a small gift.

After a 'Wedding Breakfast' with all our large party in the farmhouse kitchen (being larger than the other rooms) and few short speeches, our healths drunk in some temperance liquid, the presents inspected, our travelling costumes put on, we just had time to greet the Friends of Chelmsford Meeting and left them to partake of tea, while we drove to the station accompanied so far by Edward P Gray as Bestman; and started for Dover en route for the continent. The crossing next day was fairly calm, but the heat was most oppressive in Paris where the next few days were spent. A drive in the Bois, visits to various picture galleries, and Cathedral and churches occupied the time, but I was glad when we moved on visiting Basle, Cologne, Berne, Heidelberg up the Rhine to Interlaken, Then, lovely Lucerne, up the Rigi by little mountain railway, a grand experience for me, and then staying the night at the Hotel on the summit, we were most fortunate in having a fine morning to view the sunrise over all the snow mountains turning all the range pink.

We walked down the mountain and paddled in the stream on the way down! Another wonderful day was a visit to the Grindewald Glacier and we were able to walk in some distance, the glacier being most beautiful rainbow colours.

Going up the Grindewald on horseback was a rather trying experience to me, so unused to riding, more amusing than pleasant. We saw Giessbach waterfall illuminated in various colours, which was a lovely sight.

There are many pleasant times to remember on the tour, though in some cases the oily food did not suit either of us and we had to pay the penalty! The heat also was often very trying especially when travelling by train or diligence (foreign public stage-coach). We much enjoyed the lovely Alpine strawberries, though at one hotel we overheard the remark "only babies and fools use spoons" as we were enjoying our bowls of fruit!

Then after two weeks of travel we arrived in Chelmsford to take possession of a nice little house with pretty garden, called Orchard Villa where I took up my duties as housewife, for which I was utterly unfitted. Still we survived the ordeal - my efforts at jam-making and so on were very hopeless, the marrow and ginger jam was so solid that my husband had to break the jar to get it out! We had as our pets a very gentle collie named Nell and her fine little puppies which were allowed in our sitting room and did not improve the rugs and furniture. Father drove and rode a nice grey horse back and forth to the farm where his Father, John Marriage lived (Moulsham Lodge) or sometimes we had a skewbald pony, which was very fond of standing on its hind legs that we thought it must have been trained for a circus.

Sometimes we used his Father's horse, very tall and strong and spirited, I had to hold on to it for dear life while Father put the harness on. I think the stable at Orchard View was too low for it, and after knocking its head against the roof it got too excited to stand steady. One of the horses was Peter, very quiet and sedate, but once nearly a year after we were married I was holding it near the Moulsham nurseries when Father (ie her husband) was talking to Mr Sheerman there and two carts loaded with gravel passed. The second one drew in too close and the cart wheel was caught in our 'dog-cart' wheel so that our vehicle, poor Peter and I were all overturned in the road. When Father returned to the scene of the accident he took me into Mrs Saltmarshe's house to recover, while he picked up the broken cart and led Peter back to the Lodge where he got a low chaise and returned for me. Happily I was not much the worse except for upset nerves.

The employer of the carter paid all expenses of repairs and made most kind enquiries after me and my health. He was Colonel Disney.

Shortly after this our son Herbert John was born and I was very proud of wheeling him on the London Road as at that time it was usual to leave such work to a nursemaid and I was very pleased to hear that a gentleman who passed me commended me as a "Pattern Mother"!

I seldom left the child for a day but once we did so and went by road to Saffron Walden to a quarterly Meeting (ie of the Society of Friends) I think in September and soon after our return journey terrific rain and wind came on and we had great difficulty in finding the way. At times I held the reins while Father walked leading the horses and holding the one lamp we had to show where the edge of the road was. I think we were four hours later than we should have been, and as we neared Chelmsford, found the road full of vehicles coming away from the town where great excitement had been going on at the presentation of a jewelled sword to Sir Evelyn Wood.

The first electric lamp which had been seen in Chelmsford was lighting up Tynedale Square, and the glass was very dazzling as we approached the town.

Another dark drive I remember before the town and roadways were lighted, was when Grandfather Corder and I were coming home from a visit to Springfield, on the day of a Fete and I had to stand up and drive through the town as we were so blinded by the lights of many vehicles driving out of the town. My Father gave up in despair and thanked Providence for enabling us to get safely through the traffic – this great achievement (!) was before I was married.

My Father-in-Law John Marriage died in 1879 and we moved to the Lodge, (Moulsham Lodge Farm), where in June the next year Bernard was born, when Herbert John was two days under a year old. Herbert just started to walk and talk by his birthday. Persis followed on less than two years after, so I was kept pretty busy but with the help of a good maid we managed.

Sometimes a short holiday was a refreshment, both at Aunt Maw's beautiful home or at Aunt Anna Alexander's I have many pleasant recollections.

When Persis was still a young baby I left her in the kind care of a cousin and Father and I had a pleasant visit to Dublin and the neighbourhood, and while at Brooklawn went on a picnic to Bray; as it was early March it was perhaps unwise and after returning home I had rheumatic fever, and though not a severe attack it caused me agonizing pain. Before this date, in January 1881, we experienced a great blizzard, the depth of snow was so great that our long drive (called the Chase) was filled solid with snow to the tops of the hedges, and for weeks was impassable, except for foot passengers where a footpath was cut away. As our men refused to take the milk to the station for delivery to London, my husband and a cousin of his, undertook the task and after removing palings in the nearby field they got through, and one driving the pony and one walking before with a long pole to measure the drifts, they managed the difficult problem and sent off what I believe was the only milk to reach London from our district.

My Father had at that time removed from Writtle to Baddow where he took a nice house called the Grove. They drove into (Chelmsford) Meeting with a good mare named Alma, but she twice ran away, and after a time it became too much for my Father to drive her. My Brother was then at home until he went to settle at Bridgwater as a florist and nurseryman and had what was then a good business with great sale of mulberry trees. Henry lived in rooms there for a time until his marriage later on to Alice Impey, and I paid a pleasant visit there and had an introduction to various places of interest.

Visited Uncle F. Corder and Aunt Maria at Ipswich, taking Herbie with me – he was very interested in 'Grandpa's brother' but complained that he "said grace so fast I could not put my hands together"!

H J as a child was thoughtful and when he "wanted to say a lot of things to God asked Him to get in bed with him so he should not get cold" and "now Mummy I am afraid to move for fear I should kick him." I tried to make H understand that God was a Spirit to whom we could speak at any time.

Gerard and Arthur followed on, so we had four boys and only one girl.

I stayed at Dover with Aunt Rebecca Alexander who was most kind to me and the children. I took Arthur as a baby and one or more of the others, Father coming down at the weekend. We also went to Ireland with Arthur as a baby (about 1886) and stayed at Brooklawn with sister Mary Ann (Marriage) Allen. Had a terrible rough voyage, but happily the kindly stewardess cared for my baby as I was utterly beyond thinking of anyone but myself.

Shortly after our return Father broke his leg and had to be on crutches for some time. When he was getting better we took it into our heads to drive to Burnham-on-Crouch intending only to stay the day and took nothing with us but some sandwiches and the baby's (Arthur's) bottle. Miss Staples our lady help, and five children made up a good load and our mare, Kitty, was too weary to return that day. It being a Bank Holiday we found difficulty finding two bedrooms at an Inn and also in finding any shops open to purchase a few necessaries. At length we found one good lady who not only sold me some flannel but cut out a nightgown for the baby, which garment I made before his bedtime. The rest of us slept in our day clothes, Miss S and four children in the larger room. Father baby and I in another, and as the Inn was accommodated with a Public Bar the Bank Holiday crowd kept up a babel singing shouting till we were distracted. It was a perfect 'inferno' we did not sleep till morning dawned. We had hoped for 'a visit to the sea-side' but found the tide out when we got to Burnham-on-Crouch we all sank in the mud (and had no change of shoes).

It was very delightful to find the tide up and the sun shining for our return journey the next morning.

The next day there was a wedding at the Friends Meeting House, Ipswich to which I went. (Annette J Fry to Frederic Taylor) After the Bride and the Bridegroom had made the usual declaration they both spoke – a very unusual proceeding, but very affecting. But a commotion arose through some man (I hardly think a Friend) forcing his way through the crowd by the door saying, "I have a message from God to deliver". He made his way to the front of the Meeting and said such words as "A year ago I stood with a young bride by my side and God said to me "Within a short time she will be taken from you", and three months after she passed away". This sounded a most mournful message and I remember how I shook all over with the terrible note in the prophetic words, and it was only one short year that the bride lived. Many who attended the ceremony must have been struck by the coincidence.

Father and I visited Ackworth School once and perhaps that was the time we went on to Shields and Sunderland visiting various relatives, going to a hay making and strawberry tea at Uncle John Spence's and at Sunderland to see Uncle James Bootham Marriage.

One holiday I paid at Clacton with Gerard, and as he was a small child and not very strong, I found it a rather lonely time and my nerves were tried at the lodging, as sleeping in a downstairs bedroom, was kept awake by imagined burglars, but which proved only to be a goat which amused itself with knocking pails over!

The lady of the house amused me by saying "I do envy you your `air`" I said "Oh! don't you get any in the kitchen?" "Oh!" she replied "but yours is so nice and curly"!

Later on, Bernard developed scarlet fever and a few days later the hospital nurse took it, so that we had a second nurse in to wait on both patients, and Miss Staples and all the children except Herbert, went to stay at Walton-on-the-Naze.

My Brother (Henry Corder) was married at this time to Alice Impey and Persis was to have been a bridesmaid, but owing to the fevers, was unable to be there. Father and I were present at the ceremony but for my part we felt rather like lepers imagining that everyone was afraid of contamination!

When Bernard was well I took him to Clacton and had Miss Staples and the rest, Gerard, Arthur, Dorothy, Persis stay with us there. As Dorothy the youngest, came out with a rash soon after, I had a most distracting time when the Clacton Doctor told us "It is scarlet fever". The landlady naturally was very upset at having to disinfect the rooms and also had to go from shop to shop telling those from whom I had hired crib and pram of her fears. Ordering a cab for the conveyance of the 'invalids' paying a man 2/6^d to secure a carriage and tell the station master of the suspected case of fever, this he did not do, so I was told I was liable to a fine of £5. However all ended better than was thought possible. My husband had cleared out the little conservatory and put a crib there for Dorothy, while I slept on the dining room sofa, till the Doctor discovered that the rash was simply 'rosea' (German measles) and not scarlet fever.

Once when at Clacton with the children, we saw our first BANANAS I purchased one which was divided among the family, and we decided it tasted like a 'sleepy' pear.

We paid visit to the children when at school at Ackworth and Sidcot and had pleasant excursions from the latter place to Cheddar etc.

One of father's nieces and cousin were drowned together while on a picnic in America, they were bathing, and the bodies were not found for sometime, the search being carried out by lights of bonfires etc.

Aunt Bessie (Father's sister) was there and the loss of her niece was a great sorrow to her.

Bessie came over to visit us in England later, before her marriage to Herman Holt. They experienced the terrors of the great earthquake in San Francisco.

Father and I saw Bessie off on her return voyage (for her wedding) at Liverpool and we had a visit to Wales on our return, staying at Betws-y-Coed, which we much enjoyed. (i.e. on River Conway).

Father went three times to America during our married life and had been once before when he was about twenty and took Uncle John's wife and family over there to settle (1869). Once he sailed on the 'Servia' and the propeller was broken so the ship was in some danger. Happily I did not see the notice in the papers but the next day saw it announced "Safety of the `Servia`" Prince George of Greece was on the boat.

Once when Aunt Margaret (Father's sister) was sailing to America the ship collided with another one. She was rescued with the other passengers and cabled home the word "well" but when it reached us the word was "Hell"!

An earthquake was felt in Essex in 1884. Hardly noticeable at Chelmsford but much more severe at Colchester, where I believe, a good deal of damage was done.

Great floods in September 1888 washed away a local bridge.

In 1890 Edward, Prince of Wales, afterwards King Edward VII was present at the Essex Agricultural show and we saw him drive through the town of Chelmsford. Thought he looked very "bored" with all the decorations and rejoicing.

On Queen Victoria's 60th Jubilee we had a feast for our men and their families little knowing what was to befall us the day following. It was intensely hot and close and about 2 o'clock a dark yellow cloud came over the sky and after a great roaring sound a storm burst upon us. Thunder, lightning, hail, wind which **raged** for about quarter of an hour, meanwhile it was almost 'a darkness which might be felt' crashing of glass and windows on west side of many houses and shops in town and country round (except plate glass) were broken. A row of cottages near us had not one whole pane left, greenhouse smashed, horses ran away being frightened by the beating hail – corn was cut off as if by scissors, peapickers bruised in the fields where there was no cover – trees out clean in two as by a saw. This was called **'The Essex Tornado'** and a large sum of money was given for the relief of farmers who otherwise would have been ruined.

Another great storm later on was an unusually terrible one. My husband and I had started for a week's driving tour as we had hoped, but on putting up at an hotel in Epping Forest, the storm at night lashing without intermission from 10 to 12 o'clock, just constant crash and bang upset me so much that our 'tour' soon drew to a close, much to our disappointment.

Another occasion of note was the feeling of a great explosion at Woolwich 40 miles away, curiously enough as I was lying down at the time, I happened to be the only one who noticed the tremor and no one believed me until my husband returned from the fields, and said he had noticed all the barbed wire fencing move, and thought it might have been an earthquake.

Our dear little Paul was born five days before Christmas 1889 and was a great joy to all the family until the day before his 5th birthday when he was taken from us after a few days illness. Happily we had others who cheered our home, Marjorie next in age to him and then Irene. He was always such a sweetly affectionate brother to her, our little smiling child, of which I have no picture except in memory.

Paul died of diphtheria and eight months later Irene passed away after a painful illness of seven weeks.

Barbara was born later on in that year and helped to fill the vacant places in the hearts of her Father and Mother.

Visits were paid to us by Herman and Bessie Holt of San Francisco and later by Margaret with her husband Robert Harris of Virginia they seemed to much enjoy their visits to various English relatives - it was possible at this time that my sister-in-law Mary Ann Allen invited us to stay with her in a house she had hired at Surbiton. Father, Barbara and I were there. It was quite an interest to us to see the boating on the Thames, and one thrilling sight of a boat load of people who were run down by a steam launch. I certainly was terrified to see the people struggling in the water, but though all were dragged to safety the pink cushions from the boat, bobbing about in the river, made one dread that some human beings were still immersed.

Various other places visited and much enjoyed, such as Bournemouth with its miles of pinewoods and rhododendrons. Felixstowe on several occasions, with the usual steam boat excursions up the river Orwell to

Ipswich. To Uncle George Alexander at Tiverton and to Minehead, Ilfracombe etc.

For many years Father was one of the guardians at Chelmsford Workhouse and at Christmas time he, and sometimes our family, helped in distributing the good food to the poor souls to whom it must have been a great treat.

We also were in the field near the Union expecting to hear of the crowning of King Edward VII but had the sad news of his serious illness instead. Nevertheless the festivities were carried through as arranged though not with the pleasure we had anticipated.

Perhaps I have not referred to our Harvest Suppers which were an annual affair and much enjoyed by all concerned, both those who partook of the fine joints of roast beef and boiled mutton, with vegetables in abundance, plum puddings and pies to follow - with plenty of temperance drinks, tea, coffee, lemonade etc. Then some of the men sang songs for our great interest and amusement. 'Smoker' as he was called, was one of the favourite singers. He was only noted for singing at the Harvest Suppers, but as he came away from the Public House in the village where he lived, he would make a great to do till he got near the vicarage when he cannily changed his songs to something more soothing. The Village Parson told us this, and when he reminded 'Smoker' that the lady of the Vicarage was ill and could not stand the noise, he replied "I thought you'd like something to cheer you up."

Monica Kathleen was born April 26th 1899 and was one of my best babies - no trouble at all. I thought it was my cleverness as a Mother, but Anthony, coming later, screamed as much as any of them, so my pride was humbled!

Father and I with Marjorie and Monica had a most pleasant visit to the West of England, and stayed at Winscombe, seeing much of Arthur and Dorothy who were at school there (Sidcot Friends' School).

We visited Clevedon, Weston, Cheddar etc. Father carried Monica, the baby, round the caves. We also visited Bridgwater where my brother and his wife lived.

This visit to the West Country by Marianne was her first introduction to this part of England, and influenced her move to Burnham-on-Sea in later years..

Miss Staples, our helper in the nursery, left us soon after Tony's birth, and two helpers followed each other in the care of the young folk.

Marianne and Herbert had twelve children,

Herbert 1879 - 1940

Bernard 1880 - 1972

Persis 1882 - 1979

Gerard 1884 - 1976

Arthur 1885 - 1959

Dorothy 1887 - 1964

Paul 1889 -1894

Marjorie Emily 1892 -1980

Irene 1894 - 1895

Barbara 1895 - 1986

Monica 1899 - 1995

Anthony 1901 - 1989

Of the twelve children ten lived to old age but it is sad to realise the ten never all met. Herbert and Bernard went to Canada and never returned to England at the same time. Persis and Barbara lived in America, Gerard and Arthur served abroad in the 1914 - 18 war and Anthony was not born before the eldest boys went to Canada.

After their Father died and Marianne and the family moved to Goldrood in The Grove, Burnham-on-Sea, Somerset there is one family photograph with nine present, only Bernard missing in Canada, and Tony away at school.

Joan and her Grandmother at Goldrood, Brean

The Marriage Family – 1914 – Goldrood, Burnham

Mrs. Marriage, Herbert, Persis, Arthur, Gerard, Dorothy, Emma, Barbara, Monica.

The Stories of Herbert and Bernard Marriage

Marianne Corder and Herbert Marriage had twelve children, two died in childhood but the remaining ten lived long and eventful lives. **Herbert**, the eldest child, was born in 1879 in Chelmsford, Essex when Marianne was twenty two years old and **Bernard** followed in 1880.

Their father was anxious that they should learn to farm and Herbert went first to Kansas in the USA to help his cousin John Marriage who farmed a ranch there. Before his marriage to Marianne, Herbert (senior) had been to America taking John's wife and family out to Kansas to join John, and during his marriage to Marianne he travelled three other times to America so was anxious that his sons should travel and learn of farming in other countries.

Son Herbert farmed with cousin John in Kansas until 1902 then moved to Canada and filed a Homestead NW2 - 47 - 17 - W4 south of the town of Ryley, SE of Edmonton, the capital of Alberta. His younger sister Persis came out to Canada and acted as housekeeper for him whilst he set up home.

In 1917 Herbert ran an advertisement in an Edmonton paper for a housekeeper. The advertisement was answered by a Mrs Florence Rattray, whose husband had been killed in action during World War One. She wished to start afresh away from Edmonton, but was very apprehensive about accepting a housekeeping job. Mr Marriage met her in Ryley with horse and buggy. On the way to the farm, there was a small sod shack with grass growing on the roof. Mr Marriage turned into the driveway there, saying, "Well, this is it." Mrs Rattray, already scared at even taking the job, was ready for the next train back to Edmonton. Of course, Mr Marriage didn't carry that on too long, and took her home to his fairly nice house.

They were married the next year in 1918, with Alex Barlow and the bride's sister, May Francis as witnesses and Rev R H MacPherson as the officiating minister.

Soon after that they moved to Ontario where Herbert Victor was born. They returned to the farm at Ryley a couple years later, and Marion was born there in 1923. Dr McPherson attended them and was the family doctor until after Mr Marriage died in 1940 at the age of sixty one years.

Mr Marriage raised a lot of sheep and did his own shearing. His wife carded the wool and made quilts with the wool that was not sold. Mr

Marriage shot large numbers of coyotes that bothered the sheep, and he also brought in wild duck, prairie chicken and partridge.

A dog killing a coyote

Marian tells of the hundreds of gophers they trapped, drowned, shot and snared, and of getting one cent a tail at the height of inflation.

Mrs Marriage was not only handy at the tasks many pioneer women did - raising chickens, making all their clothes, and papering walls - she also made a lot of their furniture.

Herbert only returned to England twice, the first when a family photo is shown outside the house `Goldrood` in The Grove, Burnham-on-Sea, Somerset and again in about 1929. This is one of the rare family photos with eight of the ten living children present, Bernard the second son being already out in Canada and Tony was away at school.

Herbert died in 1940 at his home farm in Alberta aged sixty one years, leaving two children, Herbert Victor 1920 and Ruth Marian 1926.

In 1941, Mrs Marriage had a farm sale and with Marian, she moved to Victoria. Victor went into the RCAF. A few years later, they sold the farm. Mrs Marriage married again in Victoria, where she passed away in 1963 at the age of seventy one years.

Bernard Marriage

Herbert (senior) and Marianne's second son, Bernard was born in 1880 at Moulsham Lodge near Chelmsford. His father sent him to Canada in 1897 when he was seventeen, to stay with a Quaker family who farmed at Hawtry, Ontario. In 1898 he returned to England and helped his father on the farm at Moulsham Lodge until his father died in 1904.

Bernard always longed to return to Canada and he heard the appeal from Sir John A MacDonald for pioneers to go to Canada on a homesteading scheme, to establish a Dominion stretching across unclaimed Canadian land and prevent the USA from claiming this territory.

Bernard with the coyotes killed when hunting

Between 1906 and 1910 he homesteaded in Alberta and writes of his experiences there. He returned to England in 1910 and married his fiancée Ethyl Fawkes at Friends House, London and attended his Grandparents Golden Wedding celebrations.

Bernard's account of his early life in Alberta makes interesting reading and shows what a tough hard life the homesteaders experienced but the fellowship which existed, the help and sharing which was natural between them and the hard lives which their wives led.

"Without the aid of Sir John A MacDonald I might never have become a pioneer homesteader in Alberta!" Sir John's vision was a Dominion stretching from sea to sea. He wrote "the United States Government are resolved to do all they can, short of war, to get possession of the Western territory, and we must take immediate and vigorous steps to counteract them. One of the first things to be done is to show unmistakenly our resolve to build the Pacific Railway ....."

Even in a continent where the impossible has become the inevitable, the building of the railway must rank as Canada's finest achievement. Few engineering companies would dare to promise nearly 3000 miles of railroad in only four and a half years today. Yet this stupendous task was completed between 1881 and 1885.

When you consider that there was no heavy machinery in those days, that all heavy work had to be done with the aid of horses and mules and that most of the backbreaking work was done by men equipped with a pickaxe, then it seems all the more miraculous.

The route was surveyed by Sir Sandford Fleming along trails first blazed by Scottish explorers Mackenzie and Fraser. The financing was also done by the canny Scots.

The two main financiers, George Stephen (later Lord Mountstephen) and Donald A Smith, (later Lord Strathcona) made an arrangement with the government whereby they were granted land on either side of the railroad on each alternate section for a distance of thirty miles. Now the government wanted settlers and the railroad had lands to sell, so emissaries were sent to the British Isles, to Europe and to the United States.

Those who came from the United States had a distinct advantage. They were allowed to bring in duty free, a whole car load of settler's effects. Thus they had farming implements, horses and mules. Their wives could bring in their household goods and as the conditions under the Homestead Act stipulated that they need only take up residence on their land for six months of the year, that gave them the opportunity to earn good money at other jobs. All kinds of work was available. There were forests to clear, bridges to build, spur line for the railway and the breaking of land for those settlers who had arrived out west in just the clothes they stood up in.

I was young and single and filled with the spirit of adventure. I just had to see Canada and those wide open spaces for myself!

I arrived in Halifax in the spring of 1906, aged 26. How well I remember the long train ride on the Intercolonial to Montreal. The seats were hard wooden benches. Warmth was provided by a pot bellied stove and the air was strong with the smoke of 'Briar' tobacco. I had never seen anyone use a 'plug' before and I stared fascinated at this innovation.

In Montreal my chum and myself enjoyed our first good meal in Canada. I remember the steak we ate at the Windsor Hotel to this day. Back on the train again to Winnipeg and then one more change and we finally reached our destination, Wetaskiwin.

The land office informed us that the nearest land we could homestead was 60 or more miles away. There wasn't much chance of inspecting it as there was no transportation, so we took our chance and filed. My land lay about nine miles north of where the Town of Strome now stands. My chum's was further east.

He decided to buy the supplies he thought he needed for his new life. They consisted of a yoke of half broken oxen, a wagon with a double box, a plough, a stove one bed and a chair.

The railroad from Wetaskiwin was completed only as far as Daysland. We followed the construction trail alongside the track on to the south of Wavey Lake, now known as Strome.

Along the trail we saw quite a few snowshoe rabbits. My only equipment was a gun, so I managed to shoot one and we cooked it up and ate it. There were thousands of willow trees in that area. The bark must be a favourite food of the snowshoes, that snowshoe surely tasted bitter!

At a fork in the trail, my chum and I parted and I went on afoot to inspect my future home. I had no other means of guidance than the compass I carried with me. There was no road and it was snowing intermittently. The next nine miles seemed endless. It seemed to me I passed the same objects time after time. I was dog tired and finally gave up and was glad to spend the night with the people who kept the Post Office at Wavey Lake.

The next day I set off bright and early and after walking about three miles came across a little building owned by an American. His holding was the South East quarter of section 49. At last I was nearly there! Mine was the South West quarter of section 49!

I stayed with my new neighbour overnight and the next day we went searching for the surveyors mark. There was the iron stake in the ground in the centre of the property with a hole dug in each corner, to mark the boundary.

I was well pleased with my property! More than two thirds of it was nice, rolling prairie. There were a few groves of poplar and a tree known as Balm of Gilead. As I was entirely on my own I was grateful for the fact that none of the tree trunks were over five or six inches in diameter. I picked out a bluff at the north end as a suitable site for my future farm home.

Without supplies and with no one to help or guide me I did not know where to start. I decided to go and visit my brother Herbert, 27, who had been out from England for three years and who had his homestead thirty miles away at Holden. There was no road, so again I had to use a compass to find my way. After 25 miles of hard slogging I finally hit the Battle River Trail. It was merely two ruts, about six inches deep which had been made by the Conestoga wagons of the settlers. By Nightfall I was so exhausted I sought shelter at a stopping off place kept by some rough Norwegians.

What a miserable night I passed! As soon as I blew out my candle I could feel the bite of bugs. I kept re-lighting the candle and made several vain attempts to catch and kill them, to no avail.

I was glad to be on my way the next day and was soon re-united with my brother only to be pitchforked into a scene of frantic activity.

It was my first experience of a prairie fire and I hoped it would be my last. All the settlers banded together to stop the destruction. The fire was thirty miles wide. Teams of horses pulling wagons loaded with barrels of water were brought in to try to stop the fire crossing the Battle River Trail. We dampened sacks and beat at the flames while others made a hundred foot break. After 2 days and a night the fire was contained. I stayed a week at my brother's homestead and while I was there took a great fancy to a cow-pony named Fred, so I bought him. He was about four years old and had taken part in many a round up. "He's never been in harness" said my brother, rather sourly, "he won't even be able to pull a fly off a windowpane". Yet in spite of my brother, Fred turned out to be a good little horse. He cost me only thirty dollars with saddle and bridle thrown in! I returned to my own homestead and with the help of neighbours built a 12 x 16 shack. The studs were just covered with tar paper and ship lap siding and I built a sod stable to house Fred. There were days in that first bone chilling winter when it was warmer in Fred's little 'soddy' than it was in my shack.

My housekeeping was primitive in the extreme. A bag of flour, some sugar, salt and a pail of jam. For a change of diet I had some dried apples and prunes. There was a hollow at the back of my shack and after digging down 15 feet I was gratified to see the water gush. To keep out the gophers I had built a crib and dropped it down my well with a good stout lid on the top.

My horse Fred, came in very handy when it came time for me to gather in firewood for the winter. I found I could attach a rope to a bunch of poles and with a half hitch on the saddle horn he could pull it from the bush right up to the outside of my house.

I was not as smart as my neighbours when it came to building my house. The Hapgood boys had dug a hole 6 foot by 6 foot and 5 foot deep under their shack. When the really cold weather came they just lifted a trap door and went down there and hibernated like bears!

I grew quite adept at the art of bread making but ran into difficulties when it came time for me to keep the starter up to the right temperature. My personal system was to put the flour, salt, yeast and warm water in a screw top jar and place it at the bottom of my bed. My feet kept it warm all night and by the time I got my fire going my dough was all ready to go!

I pioneered the first modern deep-freeze. I cut and wrapped my meat and kept it all winter in a tin trunk at the back of the house.

We were twenty five miles from the nearest store in Daysland so I did not often get to town to stock up on groceries. When I ran out of coffee I found that I could make a good substitute by charring wheat or barley in the frying pan and then grinding it in the coffee mill.

In an emergency the deep snow presented problems so I improvised skis by cutting narrow boards which I steamed in my copper boiler and bent to shape. There was an open coal mine 8 miles away which provided me with a substance much like lignite. I found that a big chunk of this would last all night and still give off warmth. By opening up the draught in the morning I was soon warm and cosy.

It took me quite a while before I had completed the rudimentary things I needed to do to get started. I still did not have a plough so I arranged with my American neighbour for him to plough the prairie on my homestead, as I was hoping to plant wheat in the spring. Ready cash was always a problem so a friend of mine named Jack McArthur and myself decided to go and help with harvesting in the more settled parts of Saskatchewan. This meant a trip down to North Battleford which was about 200 miles away. Jack had no horse to ride so he proceeded to a nearby ranch where the owner had a bunch of half wild cayuses, or Indian ponies. He selected a white one, roped it and jumped on its back. Off it flew over the prairie with Jack clinging like a leech to its mane. I half never expected to see him again, but he brought her back only an hour later, broken. A tough little mare she proved to be. It took us four days to get to North Battleford where we arranged for stabling for our horses and stole a ride in an empty box car going in the direction of the harvest fields.

The Northern district was our destination. It was an older settled district and the first crops of wheat were ripening in the sun. I got a job working for a German with a beautiful stand of wheat. The first week was spent stooking behind the binder. Then it all had to be stacked ready for the thresher. I worked behind the thresher loading up a big wagon with a double box which contained about 60 bushels of wheat. Teams of horses worked steadily all day taking the loads a further four miles to the elevator.

The steam threshing rig was fired entirely with straw. Two lads, each with a pony attached to the ends of a long sweep, would draw the straw up to the rig where one man fed the fuel directly into the fire box. The work was long and hard. We started at daybreak and as I wearily sat behind my plodding team on my way back from the elevator, it was an impressive sight to see reddened faces of the men working away by the light of the blazing straw.

I made good use of the money I earned to buy tools and equipment for my homestead. I found though, that there was so little money around in those days and so much bartering done for food and work done in exchange for food that sometimes the possession of money was embarrassing. I had been sent a certified cheque from England and in those days we got nearly five dollars to the pound in exchange. When I cashed the cheque the bank handed me four, ten dollar gold pieces. I found when I tendered one of these in exchange for services rendered that hardly anyone could change them.

The second winter on my homestead I attached myself to Ed Dawson for the winter. Ed had a little office in Daysland where he carried on the business of Notary and Conveyancer. He lived 2 miles out and I drove him and his real estate clients backwards and forwards looking at property.

Ed found himself in a real predicament one day. He had stepped out to his pump to get a bucket of water. He had filled his bucket and stood gossiping, but evidently he must have spilled some and as he was wearing felt soled boots the water had entered the soles and his feet were frozen solid to the ground!

He had to call for someone to fetch an axe and chop him loose. That winter some Florida land promoters came to town selling lots for ten dollars. I did not invest, Florida seemed too far off then, but I know that Ed bought one and also other merchants in town. It took another sixty years to go by before I got the chance to visit Florida. There is a lot of building going on there and much land is being re-claimed, but as far as I could tell those lots are still covered with water!

I started work on my land again the following spring and had my first experience working with a team of oxen. The custom down east is to use yokes, but out west we used a harness and a specially constructed collar and harness. I used four oxen on the disk harrow and they worked just like a powerhouse. For clearing bush they had no equal. I could put a chain around a clump and while they pulled I was able to get in behind and slash away at the tree roots with an axe.

When it came to cutting grain with the binder, they put one over on me. One or two of the team would always be reaching behind for a mouthful of grain so that it was impossible to keep up any kind of motion. Somebody suggested I blindfold them. I tried that, but it did not work. With the blindfolds on they would not budge a step. Muzzling was no good with their mouths as they could still get at part of the grain so I still had to wind up getting some horses to complete my threshing.

One day when I was on my way to my brother's homestead I passed through a large settlement of European nationals. I noticed a man ploughing using ox for a furrow and there were three women pulling a rope attached to the other end of the evener. To complete my residence requirements and clear the land on my homestead, it became necessary for me to buy a heavy team of horses. The man who ran the livery stable had had his eye on Fred for some time and made me an offer on him. The offer was conditional on Fred being hitched to a cart for the drive down. I did not know if Fred would co-operate as he had never been hitched.

I rode him over to a neighbour's who owned a cart and together we put the harness on him. Then we quickly drew the vehicle up and attached it. Laying the reins over the back of the seat we jumped on. Fred made a dash and ran half a mile or so but on reflection, did not find it too bad an experience and settled down to a gentle trot.

The livery stable owner gave me the cheque and bidding Fred a fond farewell I quickly walked to the bank and cashed the cheque. Coming out of the hotel later after my first 'store bought' meal in a long time, I happened to pass the livery stable to see Fred was giving the livery man lots of trouble, so I quickly made my way home.

I thrashed thirty acres of wheat that fall but an early frost hit it and it was fit only for feed. I bought some pigs which I kept in Fred's old soddy. They made a welcome change in my diet. Coyotes were plentiful and were preying on the settlers' young calves, sheep and lambs. I bought a couple of wolf hounds and in the winter we went hunting. Beaver Lake was frozen over and one day we packed the dogs into a sleigh and drove out onto the lake.

There stood a coyote still feeding on a lamb carcass. We got as close as we could and got it in one rifle shot. Bob the stronger of the two hounds could catch and make a kill, but Fan would catch a wolf by the flank and throw it two or three times and then give up unless the collie caught up and helped her. During that winter of 1908 our total bag of wolves was 34. I had made some wonderful friends and neighbours during my homesteading days. They were all from different countries. The two Erickson boys were from Sweden, Ed Adams was up from Idaho. Davey had been a Yorkshire coal miner and the Petersons had arrived from Norway. Some families had come from the Dakotas and my chum Jack was from Collingwood in Ontario.

Like me, all these men grew to love the Similikamene Valley. Like me they all performed their homestead duties and by 1909 they were able to 'prove' and obtain title to 160 acres of good Canadian farmland. They and their families grew to love the soil as I did. I hope their descendants will keep faith and honour the pioneer heritage they left. Three boys - Jack, Richard and Robert were born whilst they lived in Alberta, then he traded his homestead for a farm at Welland near Niagara, and in 1927 sold his livestock and came to Goldrood, Brean, Somerset for a visit with his three sons.

Bernard Marriage & his second son

Persis in America and Nursing in France

The eldest daughter of Herbert and Marianne Marriage, was born in 1882 at Moulsham Lodge near Chelmsford, Essex. (The name Persis is taken from the Bible, Romans 16, Letter from Paul, Personal Greetings, "Greet my dear friend Persis, another woman who has worked very hard in the Lord"

After her father died in 1904, Persis went to Canada to housekeep for her brother Herbert at his farmstead near Ryley, Alberta, Canada. She then moved to America where Quaker relations, Elizabeth Marriage Holt and her husband Herman Holt, witnessed her appearance before a Public Notary in San Francisco, California, where she was permitted to reside.

Life with Auntie Bessie proved somewhat restrictive and so for three years she trained at University Hospital, San Francisco. By 1916 she was fully trained as a Matron or Supervisor, specialising in surgical work in men's wards.

When America entered the war she volunteered for service with the American Army Medical Corps in 1917. At first she was based in Charlotte, North Carolina, then for three weeks was based on Ellis Island, where they nursed army men coming back from the war in Europe. Then she was in Madison Square, New York. Every morning they sang the Star Spangled Banner, accompanied by Mrs Crane on the `pianner`. Then at 9.0am off to Central Park to drill under Sgt Kowles who taught them how to walk and march and stand. "Feet together: throw your chests out." "I am the best drill master in the U.S.A. I know it and you must know it."

In the afternoons they had to go to Trinity Church where Dr Read addressed them and they sang hymns and patriotic songs, then on to French lessons to prepare them for the time ahead.

Finally, training completed, the corps was sent overseas in a boat the 'Leviathan' formally a German boat the 'Vaterlant' with 14,000 passengers, officers, soldiers and nurses to France.

They enjoyed their passage, calm, smooth seas, and dances every night and shipboard flirtations going strong, but told by Mrs Crane and Col Dean that they must all be in bed by nine, otherwise they would be sent back to America, and every day at 4.30pm there was life boat drill.

Persis wrote the following in a long letter to Bessie and Herman Holt in San Francisco.

"We landed at Brest before travelling by train to Vichy. As our ship came into the harbour there were two great dirigibles, or sausage balloons, way up in the air, watching for submarines or anything of that kind.

We saw quite a few subs of the Allies in the harbour, and saw them submerge and come up again and loads of torpedo destroyers. You should see the camouflaging of some of the ships! Some are splendid and some seem absurd. The most absurd I thought was done apparently by a Cubist, a regular Harlequin ship - in pale green, pinks, lavender and blue, lozenges of colour everywhere!

But the one I liked the best was in green with a black submarine painted on it at the waters' edge, it really looked most natural. Another was painted so that it looked like a pile of old junk out in the bay, we really thought it was a mass of old boats and bits of things, but found it to be a perfectly good ship.

Next we travelled by train to Vichy. The men were taken off the boat first and we stayed on board a couple of days. One rocky part ashore looked like Cornwall and then there were gorse covered slopes. On Sunday we got up at 5.0am and were taken ashore by troop ship and twenty minutes walk to the station.

It was a lovely sunny day and we passed some fine looking peasant women with such rosy faces and snowy white coifs. I could not help noticing that there were many widows.

As we had two hours before our train, five of us took a walk to see the old Chateau and Fort. An old Frenchman who could only speak as much English as I could French took us round. He took us down to the 'oubliette' through the hole where they dropped people they desired to hear from no more! About forty years ago they found twelve corpses.

Then we got into the train, the quarter master came round with provisions, there were four of us in our compartment and we wondered if we were going to be on the train for a week. They insisted upon giving us eight large loaves, six or seven cans of corned beef, two of pork and beans, two of tomatoes and one of jam. Most of us had only an enamel cup but one of us had some cutlery. We opened the cans with an old pair of nail scissors. We ate pork and beans out of our cups and then wiped them out with bread.

The countryside was lovely, banks of primroses, cowslips, bluebells, bee orchids, lovely winding rivers banked with glorious vivid green trees and tidy little fields with hedges round them. Interesting cottages and rosy cheeked old peasant women and now and again an old man, never a young man, boys of 15 doing the ploughing and few animals. It was hard to imagine the devastation in other parts of France.

The journey was very slow and we stopped often. People came out and cheered us "Vive les Americains", though I heard that others wished we had never come otherwise it would have been over sooner.

After two days, we stopped off in the country where there was a water faucet, you should have seen the rush for towels and soap and everyone Doctors, nurses, enlisted men, waiting their turn to get a real wash, some men even got to shave.

Finally we arrived at our destination and were met by Major of Chief Nurse of Unit 1 Bellvue."

The Unit was based at Royat, near Claremont Ferrand and their hotel was 'De France and Angleterre', where they had to set to and clean and scrub everything in order to turn it into a hospital. On June 16th the first patients came there, British Tommies.

Until the hotel at Claremont was fit to be used, the nurses had to help out in other hospitals which were understaffed. They saw many troops in differing uniforms, Americans, French, Alpine Chasseurs and British. She felt most affected by those who had their faces shattered and saw quite a few cases from gas attacks. Some of the nurses were sent right up to the front but Persis remained at Claremont Ferrand.

The photographs below show the American nurses at mealtime

Persis is on the far left of this photograph

In this photograph, Persis is in the centre turning to face the camera

Whilst at this base Persis was able to get travel passes and provided it said `War Zone` on the pass, the nurses made some extensive visits. She sent home many postcards of her visits.

Persis went by train to Paris staying at Hotel Mary, 9 Rue Greffuhle, where she was able to get bed and breakfast and eat at the WYCA. In Paris on a Monday, everything was closed but she managed to get to Notre Dame and the Luxembourg Gardens. In the evening she went to the Champs Elysee theatre to see Whiz Bang-344 Art Show. She wanted to go to Verdun but it was an all night journey with an early morning change of train but she met an American professor from the University of Beaune who told her of his trip there to Dead Man's Hill. He said there was not an inch of ground not churned over and over again. The forest was no more, not a tree left standing. The village nearby was no longer there, just a hole in the ground. He went through some of the Crown Princes' trenches where they had good dugouts, one large tiled room with comforts in. The Germans expected to accomplish much here but the French said `they shall not pass` - and they didn't. Dead Man's Hill is now covered with violets, you cannot step without treading on them.

From Paris, Persis managed to get to Rheims. Between Chateau Thierry and Rheims she saw at least twenty five villages, each one a mass of ruins. Many trenches all along, but being filled up fast and people coming back to plant their vineyards, great champagne country. From the window they could see graves out in the fields. Some of the men they travelled with had been further out in the country and said there were still dead German bodies lying there.

In Rheims, Persis visited the Cathedral but the city was nothing but a ruin. It had been a wonderful building but looked ruined beyond redemption. A few people were returning to the city, a few hotels had been patched up and little fruit stalls had opened up.

They took a truck out to the old Hindenburg line and went down one of the old trenches and saw the dugouts where the men had slept and eaten. She warns the friend (another nurse) who she was writing to – "If you go there for goodness sake do not touch anything, there are many unexploded shells about and a couple of weeks ago a soldier was killed and a nurse hurt, because the boy fooled with a shell and it went off."

Back in Paris she went to see the `Patheon de la Guerre` a circular painting representing all the Allies with hundreds of people shown and it is said they are all real people and can be recognised. Edith Cavell is shown in the middle of England.

At the end of the war Persis stayed on for some time voluntarily helping nurse people struck down by a `flu epidemic'. When she decided to leave the nursing corps she requested to return to England and visit her Mother, Marianne Marriage who was now old and living with her daughters at Goldrood, Brean. She then spent a year touring in France, Italy and England, finally returning to San Francisco where she ran an antique shop.

In 1963 she returned to England, living in a bungalow at Brean and for the last six years of her life, lived in a Quaker sheltered house at Winscombe near the Quaker school Sidcot, where many of the family had been at school. She died in Weston in 1979 aged 97.

Gerard and Arthur Marriage

And the Friends' Ambulance Unit

Gerard, born on January 29th 1884 and Arthur 1885 were the fourth and fifth children of Herbert and Marianne Marriage and were born at Moulsham Lodge near Chelmsford.

Gerard was apprenticed as a motor mechanic at Marconi's in Chelmsford and Arthur trained as a nurseryman at Cheals Nursery. He later moved to Wincanton in Somerset and his sister Dorothy looked after him as a housekeeper. In 1904 his father died and when his grandmother also died in 1914, Arthur found the house in Burnham-on-Sea, where his mother and family moved to, calling the house Goldrood, after their old Essex house.

Compulsory military service was introduced in World Wars I and II and Friends had to appear before a tribunal to justify their stand as conscientious objectors, but when war broke out in 1914 Gerard and Arthur both joined the Friends Ambulance unit in France, where they served as drivers and ambulance men.

British Red Cross Unit sent to Italy

Gerard continued to work for the Ambulance Unit until 1915, when he joined the British Red Cross Unit in Italy, which Austria had invaded. In 1916 the first British tanks were deployed in Europe, and Gerard serviced these as well as trucks and ambulances. The Unit was formed in England and vehicles were sent out and driven across France to Italy.

Dear Mater,

I have not had a letter through from you to our new address, but I guess there is probably one on the way. As you may imagine we have been travelling around this country and will shortly be doing some more! I think my last scrawl to you was from Padua. Now I am up here in Milan doing some buying to the tune of £200 - £300 to refit our repair shop, as we lost nearly everything, so you see your prodigal son is getting quite a linguist. I lost every blessed thing except the clothes I stood up in and my camera which was hanging round my neck. I suppose I must consider myself lucky to have got away with a whole skin!

I should like to tell you the full story of our recent movements, but one has to be jolly careful of what one says, but I believe your English papers give a fairly good account of things.

I am afraid I shall have to order a fresh uniform; I suppose it will come to about £40. I don't know if the BRC are going to do anything about it as I'm afraid my account will not stand up to it. I had my kit done up in three lots as I thought I would be sure of saving some. I put the first lot in one of our best cars, and the other two, into my little two seater. The first got a few miles and the edge of the road gave way and the car went into the ditch and turned over.

We had three cars in dock but scrambled all together and got them ready and all moved off at 3am. We had to leave one car behind and two had been lost by shells. The first 500 yards were fine, but then the next took two hours. The main road with ditches each side absolutely crammed with vehicles of all sorts, lorries loaded up with stores, huge tractors drawing guns, ambulances, horse carts, bullock wagons with peasants on board, with all their worldly goods, sometimes including pigs, geese, calves etc. Mule carts galore and any little space filled with pack mules and civilians on foot worming their way through the muddy road. At the first turning we got off onto a bye road to make better speed for a mile or so but then got into traffic and had to crawl. An hour or two further on we came upon the car we had scrambled together and the back axle had broken.

We stayed sometime trying to get a tow, by now it had started to rain in torrents, so I started off in my little Ford to try to catch up with our front cars but was met by a motor cyclist saying they had gone on past the next town, so I had to turn back against the stream and collect the driver and attendant who had stayed with the car and all our personal kit.

So off we set with four in my two seater, got nearly to the town and were turned away by the military, couldn't get through as well......... you can guess. We had to make a big detour south.

The night before we had left on our journey, we were staying at a small Austrian cottage and had got the conked cars under the safest wall because we were way up in the mountains just behind the front lines, under quite lively shell fire. I had gone up in the morning, in my two seater, to fit a dynamo on one of the conked cars. It is quite interesting trying to make small adjustments to things like dynamo and magnetos under such circumstances, with objectionable things making objectionable noises to right and left of one, and throwing objectionable mud at you! You are almost sure to duck your head instinctively just as you are fixing a screw or nut. We got that car fixed in time and I had orders to move at midnight.

Finally we found another larger car with a chap at the wheel who seemed somewhat tired – he'd been at the wheel for 36 hours. We carried on for an hour or two, waking each other up, then word was sent back that we must abandon this and walk as we were still some way from the river and daylight would soon be there. I never was fond of strolling along country roads at 5am with refractory mules liable to tread on ones' toes at any minute!

One of our party was wounded and had about five miles to do on foot, partly on one leg and crutches, and partly carried on a stretcher. Just before dawn, we caught up with one of our busses and climbed in, and we got to the river bank. I found the remains of a cold plum pudding and some tinned sausages, which the driver had had sent out from the house. My but that was good, as I had only had a somewhat dirty bottom crust of an army loaf of bread to chew for a good many hours.

We passed over the river on the roof of the bus and now moved along a lot better, and after driving all morning, came to our first meeting place (it's now in 'other hands') and got petrol and food and a little sleep on an hotel floor. In the middle of the night, called up and on we go again; driving all the rest of the night and in the morning arrived at Padua. Had two days rest here and bought some clothes and had a much needed shave and bath. Soon got moving again to the place where you were told to send letters.

This morning being Sunday and no business to be done, three others of our people and myself were invited and given a box at the Scala Theatre, where a big distribution of medals was taking place. It was very interesting, and also in parts very sad, as there were a number of recipients crippled for life, and a number of medals were presented to mothers and fathers for some killed in action.

Well this is such a fine literary effort, compared with my usual one that I hope my good friend, the Censor, will find nothing to object to. I have not given you the more interesting details of our little jaunt, because I thought he might tear the whole thing up, but only the plain unvarnished facts, such as you get in the reliable press, except that they seem to be allowed to give more details.

    Much love,

     Yours ever,

      "Gee"

In October 1918, the Italians made great military advances, and in November the Armistice was signed. The Unit drove back to England but Gerry stayed on for some time, helping to repair vehicles and establish Italian communications.

Stretcher Bearers' Drill

He returned to England, settled in Haverford West, Pembrokeshire, where he was looked after by his sisters, Marjorie and Monica, from 1920-1925. His first wife died and he married Amelia Skone Wilkins. In 1947 he retired and they went to live in Brean, Somerset at 'Beachwood', built on part of the land of Goldrood.

Arthur joined Gerard in the Friends Ambulance Unit in France in 1914. He served as an ambulance driver and stretcher bearer, but was so affected by the horrors he saw in the trenches in France, that he left the Unit and joined the Somerset Light Infantry, serving in Egypt and Albania.

For this he was thrown out of the Society of Friends, but after the war this was reconsidered and he was allowed to rejoin.

After the war, Arthur maintained his horticultural career and had a fruit tree nursery, 'Kennington Nurseries' in Ashford, Kent.

Later, he moved back to Somerset and had a nursery garden at West Lyng, then retired to live at Lower Merridge in the Quantock Hills. Arthur married Edith Rookledge in 1923. Both he and his wife were great nature lovers. Edith was a fungi expert and did many beautiful drawings of mushrooms and toadstools. Arthur loved birds and studied them in great detail. He made delightful plaques cut into plaster, and painted birds on the raised surfaces. In particular, his paintings of birds of prey were most impressive and many of these were sold in Taunton.

Arthur died in Bridgwater Hospital in 1959.

The Main Stairway, Goldrood

The Bacon Closet

The Larder

Mr. Lockwood Gardening